A MUSLIM
AND A
CHRISTIAN
IN DIALOGUE

A MUSLIM AND A CHRISTIAN IN DIALOGUE

**Badru D. Kateregga
and David W. Shenk**

HERALD PRESS
Scottdale, Pennsylvania
Waterloo, Ontario

Library of Congress Cataloging-in-Publication Data
Kateregga, Badru D.
    A Muslim and a Christian in dialogue / [by Badru D. Kateregga and David W. Shenk].
      p. cm.
    Includes bibliographical references (p.).
    ISBN 0-8361-9052-1 (alk. paper)
    1. Islam—Relations—Christianity. 2. Christianity and other religions—Islam. I. Shenk, David W., 1937- . II. Title
    BP172.K346 1997
    261.2'7—dc21   96-49805

The paper used in this publication is recycled and meets the minimum requirements of American National Standard for Information Sciences—Permanence of Paper for Printed Library Materials, ANSI Z39.48-1984.

A MUSLIM AND A CHRISTIAN IN DIALOGUE
Copyright © 1997 by Herald Press, Scottdale, Pa. 15683
    Published simultaneously in Canada by Herald Press,
    Waterloo, Ontario, N2L 6H7. All rights reserved
First edition published by Uzima Press (1980) and
Wm. B. Eerdmans Publishing Co. (1981)
Library of Congress Catalog Number: 96-49805
International Standard Book Number: 0-8361-9052-1
Printed in the United States of America
Book and cover design by Jim Butti

08 07 06 05 04 03 02   10 9 8 7 6 5 4

To order or request information, please call
1-800-759-4447 (individuals); 1-800-245-7894 (trade).
Website: www.mph.org

To
Faridah
who is Badru's wife
and
Grace
who is David's wife

Contents

Foreword I

As a Muslim it would be unreal for me not to be impressed by the bravery of two authors who write with honesty, tolerance, courtesy, and politeness on the fundamental matters of Islam and Christianity. They are able to express the stand of each on matters of faith in God and Prophethood, the meaning of evil and sin and more, without attempting to make the reader believe in the rightness of one faith over the other. Badru Kateregga and David Shenk may be among the first to attempt such a dialogue, which lets the reader be the sole judge of the message behind the contents.

Sheikh Zakariya Razy (not Rhaze) in one of his books wrote about the different schools of thought in Islam, stating the merits of each one without prejudice over the other. He did not suggest, for instance, the rightness of the convictions of the Al-Ash-ariya over the Qadariya or the Qadariya over the Jabariya and vice versa, although he himself belonged to Al-Ash-ariya. His book was a comparative study of the different schools of thoughts and sects in Islam. All scholars irrespective of their convictions received it with admiration. Badru Kateregga and David Shenk have gone a step further by undertaking a similar discussion on the two religions themselves.

This is a worthy attempt between these two scholars who with good intentions in their hearts thought of bringing out in one volume the creeds of two of the world's main religions. Each in his own faith has stated exactly what his religion stands for without compromise, despite the response at the end of each chapter. Each has conveyed in language that is as straightforward as possible the stand of the Scriptures.

Badru Kateregga, lecturer by profession, presents the facts as he knows them from the Qur'an and the traditions (*Sunnah*) of the Prophet Muhammad (peace be upon him) without elaboration or attempt to convince the reader.

David Shenk, pastor and a university lecturer, states his facts in the language of a preacher which carries little attempt to convince, yet must work to avoid doing so. In spite of this slight imbalance in the dialogue, it is hard to read this book and not admire the motives of the two writers in undertaking such a task. What was it? Could it have been an academic exercise or a call to present to the reader the religion of God?

Maybe the reader will see it this way—presenting the two religions from a faithful Muslim and a faithful Christian for the readers to compare. Faith is a state of belief which has very strong fixation. Comparison is useful with two comparable facts or sets of alternatives. In the religious faith, the principle of comparability or alternating with another faith hardly exists, if at all. Where there are similarities, they are always preceded by conditions and *buts.* To the Muslim the miraculous birth of Jesus and the virginity of Mary are part of the faith. God said "be" and Jesus became.

"Thus God creates whatever he wills. He commands a thing to be and it is" (Qur'an 3:46). To the Christian the miracle is not only of the birth but also the descent of God into humanity. The two sets of faiths are incomparable. One is of a man and prophet being decreed by God to be born miraculously, as Adam was created out of nothing, so to speak. The other is of the same person as Son of God, whose extension into a human form was to come through being born by a woman.

The Oneness of God presented by Badru insists on God being One in His own Oneness. There is neither extension nor incarnation. His coming to persons is His omnipresence in them and with them at every time and every place. The Christian unity of God is in the Trinity, the three-in-one. There is no Oneness without God's extension unto his Son and the Holy Spirit. God's coming to humans was in flesh of a human being, in the way of the human life and habits. Christians believe that the Trinity is always in their presence. This way of belief is woven throughout the book. The principle of original sin does not exist in Islam. Persons are born in primordial innocence. Adam was forgiven and cleansed of sin before his descent to earth, so Badru explains. Sin is never inherited in Islam. People are judged by their merits.

When we accept this understanding of the uncompromising dialogue of these two authors, we can appreciate the value of this book. The admirable factors for us all are the tolerance and respect demonstrated in this work by each writer responding to the other's chapter in politeness and restraint, without arguments or claim for justification.

For those who want to know Islam, this book gives them opportunity to read of it in its most fundamental form. For those who want to learn about Christianity, the book presents to them in simple language the creeds of Christian faith. It appears to me that the two authors agreed to present two books in one; the bonus is that each responded to the witness of the other. Maybe that was their meeting ground. Given that both are concerned with teaching comparative religion, that could have been a natural meeting ground.

The Prophet Muhammad (peace be upon him) used to debate with Christians in a kind atmosphere. He never showed the hardness or severity which characterized his debates with polytheists (*mushrikun*) and idol worshipers. He argued on the basis of Scriptures as he was told in the Qur'an, 'God asked Jesus, son of Mary: "Did you ask the people to take you and your mother as two gods beside God?" Jesus answered: "Praise be to you alone, I had not said but that which I was commanded to say. You surely know whether I am guilty of such blasphemy, for you know all that is in my thoughts and I know none of what is in yours. You alone are omniscient. I did convey to them that which you commanded me to convey, namely that they ought to worship God alone, my lord and their Lord. In their midst I have been a witness unto you throughout my life" ' (Qur'an 5:116-118).

—*Sheikh Abdulla Saleh Farsy*
Chief Kadhi of Kenya

Foreword II

Was it wise to invite a foreword to this venture from one so fully committed to its themes and purpose? It might have been well to ask a commendation from a sociologist. She might have withheld it on the ground that the text was so heavily theological and seemed unaware of the sanctions of community and communal consciousness which so largely determine the mental positions we take even when they are irenic.

Perhaps it might have been preferable to get an introductory note from a Marxist who would, no doubt, have remarked that the element of realism about economic structures and their part in religious attitudes was missing. He would certainly have noticed the strong individualism of the concepts of evil, especially on the Islamic side; he might have wondered about the sanguine view implied about the innocence of structures, including those of religion itself.

Perhaps a preview should have been entrusted to some master of African culture and anthropology to bring the whole more squarely into what President Kenyatta, in a notable pioneer study, called *Facing Mount Kenya*. Such an introducer would have noted that the field of symbol and ritual and ancestors was strangely absent from the discussion. She would probably have queried the ready reliance on conceptual thinking and verbal exposition. She might have wondered whether both authors had been too unsuspectingly Western in their approach. But then, she would have said, all dialogue is apt to be that way.

Perhaps this foreword should have been written by someone

like Bertolt Brecht, the German poet and playwright of the forties and fifties. Brecht was once asked what he would suggest for his tombstone and replied, "Write that I was an uncomfortable person, and that I expect to remain so." He had that radical sense which bracingly questioned all religious assurance, yet did so with a wistfulness that made unbelief sensitive and warm.

How can we be so sure of authority when God seems so elusive? Have our convictions about revelation really reckoned with how baffling the experiences of our mortality are? Are we honest enough in our ideal claims about the *Ummah* "transcending ethnic and cultural barriers," or the church "embracing all humankind"? In our doctrines of transcendence—whether what Badru Kateregga calls "the absolute legal sovereignty of Allah," or what David Shenk calls "the infinite love of God"—have we adequately measured the secular perplexities which cannot find their relevance amid the apparent ultimates of contemporary history?

Have we believers in God's presence sufficiently understood the secular experience of God's absence—or God's hiddenness? Perhaps most of all, in our assurance about the human race—whether Islamic person, perfectible and merely frail, or Christian, graced in Christ and redeemable—have we truly realized how demonic people may be? Jewish thinking, such as Martin Buber's, might sober Muslims and Christians in this regard.

Perhaps we should ask a poet to do a frontispiece—Pasternak perhaps, or Walter De la Mare, or Wole Soyinka. Poetry has a way of refining the prose of our ideas into the feel of mystery and thus takes the mind into the heart. Conversation might then be less articulate and serviceable but also more intimate and open. Perhaps we should ask a Buddhist to write our foreword and bring a quite contrasted angle of vision to our relationships.

Valuable and salutary as any of these alternatives would be, the authors have chosen me, and I am happy to serve. I fully share their hopes and concerns; it is a privilege to commend the authors to a wide range of readers around the globe. However, in doing so I want to have in mind the queries and misgivings of the conceivable other choices for this role. I hope all readers will have an awareness too of how these other perspectives relate to what they find.

Given the pattern the authors have followed, two impressions emerge. The first is how far we have come from polemic and barren controversy. To use Peter's phrase in his New Testament letter, "this is thankworthy." It is important that the approach these authors model deepen and widen among us. There are still sad areas of what might be called "fanatical consciousness" which remain impervious to love and honesty. Rejectionism has a way of growing by psychic factors, feeding on itself and stiffening its obduracy. We can never be confident that we have overcome it; we must always be dedicated to doing so.

The other impression is that consciousness within religious establishments of faith and practice, though free from the fanatical, can still remain unresponsive to meaning from outside. This in a way is the frustration of dialogue. As in the present study, we each state our case. We indicate differences. We disentangle misunderstandings. We reaffirm positions. We maintain politeness. We even repent. What then? For the most part, we stay in our positions, sometimes failing to take in what the other means. Response sometimes reveals that we are not responding. There are numerous examples here. To query God's resting on the seventh day on the ground that he is almighty and needs no rest; to note that it may have been Jibril in the burning bush in comment on the theme of God in history; to disown anthropomorphism in discussion of analogy—these indicate a nonpenetration of meaning. The situation is mutual.

That seems to suggest that now we should try to move away from position statements with courteous rejoinders. We should aim with continuing courtesy to develop areas of experience which—while involving what is at issue in the familiar divergencies of view—focus it vitally in terms which we both experience and which neither of us sponsor as sole proprietors. This may allow us to escape from the formalism of dogma and positional thinking and into genuine enterprise of mind and spirit. Perhaps I can put the point by saying that we will then get our bearings by our compass of faith instead of staying believers by a tether of authority.

In confessing transcendence, for example, we might transcend our familiar custodianship and explore the way humans absolutize their structures in history, even their religious ones, and so commit the *Shirk* of idolatry. Then we may see the theme of unity and

Tauhid as essential, not propositional—as having to do, not with number, but with the effective rule of God, relativizing all else. We might also explore sin in the world, as the late Dr. Muhammad Kamil Husain did in Cairo, not in abstract terms about Adam's lapse of rebellion, but in the concrete form of communal pride, pseudo-loyalties, and corporate expedience which we all experience today.

I suppose it would be right to say that the central controversy between Islam and Christianity has to do with the distancing or otherwise between the divine and the human. It is this which pervades all the themes of revelation, prophetic vocation, the ways of divine mercy, the categories of law and love, the degree of *kenosis* (or self-emptying) in creation itself on God's part, and the question of Jesus and the cross. It is urgent for us to live together in the depth of these issues, neither foreclosing them by anathemas nor obscuring them by neglect. Rather we should let them press more fully upon us through our openness to common action in the day-to-day scene and by our readiness to think second or even third thoughts about the responses we first instinctively make.

No doubt not all will discover this sense of vocation. Many readers will find what they seek in these chapters, which is a quiet reiteration of what they believe. They will wholeheartedly welcome it by half! It may even serve useful purposes that way. It is important that we know where we are and have a careful, respectful statement of our case. Others will wish that the brief rejoinders to the position chapters had been either less predictable or more full.

The task to which Kateregga and Shenk set their hand is continuing business. Readers will understand more clearly because of the authors' patient frankness and sincerity in approach and in exposition. The authors have presented both the assets and the liabilities of the relationship between their faiths. Africa, by and large, has a better tradition of interfaith coexistence than other continents. What the African ethos will yet do with the external heritage of church and mosque belongs to the future, but that future is steadily being shaped in decisions of the present. Authors like ours will best be rewarded by those decisions they help readers make, each in his and her own integrity of mind and heart.

—*Bishop Kenneth Cragg*

Acknowledgments

We express our sincere gratitude to Mr. A. A. El-Maawy, Education Officer, Ministry of Basic Education, Kenya, and director of *Tabliqh* and *Daawa* (Religious Affairs) in the Supreme Council of Kenya Muslims (LSUPKEM), for reading the manuscript and making valuable suggestions. We are also indebted to Sheikh Ali Darani, Qadhi of Mombasa, for reading through some of our chapters and making various comments. We also thank Dr. Omar Hassan Kasule of Mulago Hospital, Uganda; Sheikh Ahmad Mukasa, Secretary for Religious Affairs in the Uganda Muslim Supreme Council; Sheikh Edrisa Songolo, Deputy Qadhi, Busoga Province, Uganda; Mr. Ismail Gyagenda of Makerere University; Sheikh Burhan Ssebayigga of Islamic Development Bank Jedda, Saudi Arabia; and Mr. Atiq Quraishy, Ministry of Higher Education, Kenya; for insight and for answering a number of inquiries we put to them.

We further acknowledge our indebtedness to the Reverend Dr. Kenneth Cragg and Professor William Bijlefeld, who read portions of the manuscript and made valuable suggestions. Others who gave counsel, particularly on the Christian portions of the manuscript, included the Reverend Dr. Peter Ipema, former general adviser for the Islam in Africa Project (IAP), and the current adviser, Reverend Dr. James P. Dretke. Mr. Silas Wanda, project officer for the IAP, also contributed counsel.

Other IAP advisers who read the early versions of the manuscript included Reverend Richard Moller-Petersen, Sierra Leone; Reverend Donald Bobb, Ivory Coast; and Reverend Nils Ronnbeck, Kenya. Reverend and Mrs. Ron Ward of the African Christian

Church and Schools as well as Mr. Fred Kniss, Reverend Roy Brubaker, Miss Bertha Beachy, and Reverend Paul Zehr of the Mennonite Church were most helpful. Reverend Isaiah Muita of World Vision International also assisted.

We are especially indebted to our wives, Faridah and Grace, for carefully typing the manuscript and for their constant encouragement and advice. We are grateful to other family members for patiently bearing with us while we prepared this work.

The Reverend Horace Etemesi of Uzima Press Limited, Kenya, put in many hours of consultation with us; as publisher of an earlier edition of this book, he certainly went beyond the call of duty. Similar appreciation is extended to Mr. Nathan O. Kayonde, whose theological perspectives were constructive.

Kenyatta University College, Nairobi, Kenya; and Eastern Mennonite Board, Salunga, Pennsylvania, deserve special mention. Both have contributed resources in their respective ways for the completion of this book.

—*Badru D. Kateregga*
David W. Shenk

Authors' Note on Transliteration
We have deliberately omitted some marks in the transliteration of Arabic words in the interest, we hope, of our readers who are not familiar with Arabic.

—*B.D.K*
D.W.S.

Authors' Preface

Hundreds of millions of Muslims and Christians are each other's neighbors. The faithful in both communities believe they have been called by God to be witnesses, yet they seldom hear each other's witness. The collision of their histories has created walls which separate. Although both communities worship the same God and seek to be the people of God, they seldom listen to one another.

This book is an attempt by a Muslim and a Christian to witness and to listen. We, the authors, are close friends. We have taught together in the Department of Philosophy and Religious Studies at Kenyatta University College, Kenya. Badru Kateregga, a Muslim, taught Islamic history and theology. David Shenk, a Christian, taught Christian history and theology. We have taught comparative religion in a team-teaching relationship. Often the team-teaching was a dialogue, a witness from one faith to another in the presence of our students.

We have sensed that the dialogue in witness between Muslims and Christians is serious. The issues are profound. They are about the basic questions of the human situation. This means that in the hearing and the giving of witness in dialogue there is pain. Perhaps we mutually fear the pain. Perhaps that is one reason Muslims and Christians seldom speak with one another concerning faith.

Nevertheless, we authors believe witness in dialogue is vital. We need to learn to speak with one another from within our respective communities of faith. That is what we have tried to do in this book. We have not minced words. We have spoken with candor. We have each attempted to be as faithful as possible to the respective witness to which we each believe God has called us.

The book is divided into two sections. The first part is written by Badru as a Muslim faith witness. The second part is written by David as a Christian faith witness.

Each part consists of twelve chapters. At the end of each chapter is a response from the one to whom the witness is being given. That is to say, at the end of each of the twelve chapters of Muslim witness, there is a Christian response; similarly at the end of each of the twelve chapters of Christian witness, there is a Muslim response. In some cases, there is a further statement of clarification following the response.

We have written as individuals and as friends. We are personally responsible for what we have said, for ultimately faith witness is intensely personal. Nevertheless, we do speak from within particular faith communities. Badru has relied heavily on the Qur'an for his presentation, and David has based his writing primarily on the Bible. Badru witnesses from within the Sunni experience. David gives his witness from within the evangelical Protestant experience. Yet both have attempted to be sensitive to the total faith communities from which their respective witnesses emerge.

The theological and practical dimensions of faith explored in this book are not exhaustive but are indications of the nature of the encounter between Christians and Muslims. The book represents a comparative theology which we hope is free of judgmentalism and bias. We have tried to stick to our self-imposed rule: Don't interpret my faith for me!

We believe this book will provide constructive insights for any Muslims or Christians who want to understand the nature of the two great faith communities of Islam and Christianity. We hope it can be used as a basis for discussion and dialogue between Christians and Muslims.

We also believe this book would be valuable for students in upper high school, in Islamic and Christian theological schools, and as an introductory book for university students.

Muslims are usually uncomfortable with Christians writing about Islam. Similarly Christians seldom identify with Muslim interpretations of Christianity. This book, jointly authored by a Muslim and a Christian, has been written under the glaring light of mutual presence. Every word we have written has been honed by knowledge that we are working together. Honesty, kindness, and sensitivity have therefore been absolutely necessary.

—Badru D. Kateregga
David W. Shenk

A MUSLIM
AND A
CHRISTIAN
IN DIALOGUE

A Muslim Prayer

In the name of God, Most Gracious, Most Merciful.
Praise be to God,
The Cherisher and Sustainer of the Worlds;
Most Gracious, Most Merciful;
Master of the Day of Judgment.
Thee do we worship,
And Thine aid we seek.
Show us the straight way,
The way of those on whom
Thou hast bestowed Thy Grace,
Those whose (portion)
Is not wrath,
And who go not astray.

(The *Fatiha* which is the opening chapter of the Qur'an)

This is the prayer which is repeated by faithful Muslims at least seventeen times a day during the five experiences of corporate prayer.

A Christian Prayer

Πάτερ ἡμῶν ὁ ἐν τοῖς οὐρανοῖς,
ἁγιασθήτω τὸ ὄνομά σου,
ἐλθέτω ἡ βασιλεία σου,
γενηθήτω τὸ θέλημά σου,
  ὡς ἐν οὐρανῷ καὶ ἐπὶ γῆς.
Τὸν ἄρτον ἡμῶν τὸν ἐπιούσιον δὸς ἡμῖν
  σήμερον·
καὶ ἄφες ἡμῖν τὰ ὀφειλήματα ἡμῶν,
  ὡς καὶ ἡμεῖς ἀφήκαμεν τοῖς ὀφειλέταις
  ἡμῶν·
καὶ μὴ εἰσενέγκῃς ἡμᾶς εἰς πειρασμόν,
  ἀλλὰ ῥῦσαι ἡμᾶς ἀπὸ τοῦ πονηροῦ.

Our Father who art in heaven,
Hallowed be thy name.
Thy kingdom come,
Thy will be done,
On earth as it is in heaven.
Give us this day our daily bread;
And forgive us our debts,
As we also have forgiven our debtors;
And lead us not into temptation,
But deliver us from evil.

For thine is the kingdom and the power
and the glory, for ever. Amen.

(Matthew 6:9-13)

This is a prayer which Jesus Christ (the Messiah) taught his disciples to pray; it is sometimes called the Lord's Prayer or the Family Prayer.

23

PART I
THE MUSLIM WITNESS

In the Name of Allah, the Compassionate, the Merciful.

1
There Is No God but Allah

THE MUSLIM WITNESS

Islam means total submission to the commands and will of Allah,[1] the only true God. The first and greatest teaching of Islam is proclaimed by the *Shahada* (confession): *La ilaha illa 'llah Muhammadun rasal Allah.* This means: There is no god but Allah, and Muhammad is the apostle of Allah. It is this very confession which, once uttered sincerely and followed completely, makes one a real Muslim. It is this Shahada which leads a Muslim throughout his life.

Islam is a strictly monotheistic religion. The key *Surah* (chapter) in the Qur'an testifies to Islam's monotheism.

Say: He is Allah, the One!
Allah, the eternally Besought of all!
He begetteth not nor was begotten.
And there is none comparable unto Him. (Qur'an 112)

A Muslim must believe in One God (Allah). Belief in Allah is the very basis of the *al-Din* (religion) of Islam. Allah Himself has commanded, "And cry not unto any other god along with Allah. There is no god save Him" (Qur'an 28:88). Elsewhere we read, "Surely pure religion is for Allah only" (Qur'an 39:3).

God is One

No human language is good enough to describe God, for nothing else is like Him. God's nature is beyond our conception. Nevertheless we do know He is One. Allah, the One true God, is not far from us, for He is with us always. The Qur'an says, "We (God) are nearer to him (man) than his jugular vein" (Qur'an 50:16).

Allah is One, and only He is God. He is the only one worthy of worship. Allah said, "Choose not two gods. There is only One God. So of Me, Me only, be in awe" (Qur'an 16:51).

All other things and beings which humans both know and know not are God's creatures, and we must recognize that all forms of God's creation are not in any way to be compared to Him. "I am only a warner, and there is no God save Allah, the One, the Absolute" (Qur'an 38:66).

In another verse God says, "Follow that which is sent down unto you from your Lord, and follow no protecting friends beside Him" (Qur'an 7:3).

So, because God is One, no one else can share even an atom of His divine power and authority. God alone possesses the attributes of divinity. Because God is One and One only, to associate any being with God is both a sinful and an infidel act. Islam makes clear that God has no son, no father, brother, sister, wife, or daughters. The pre-Islamic (*jahiliyya*) idea of calling goddesses daughters of Allah (al-Manat, al-Lat, al-Uzza) was condemned by the Prophet (peace be upon him) for Allah has no need for daughters. In His unity, God is not like any other person or thing that can come to anyone's mind. His qualities and nature are conspicuously unique. He has no associates.

God the Creator
A Muslim must believe that Allah is the Creator of the universe and everything in it. The Qur'an says, "He it is Who created the heavens and the earth in truth" (Qur'an 6:73). It adds,

> Lo! your Lord is Allah Who created the heavens and the earth in six days, then mounted He the Throne. He covereth the night with the day, which is in haste to follow it, and hath made the sun and the moon and the stars subservient by His command. His verily is all creation and commandment. Blessed be Allah, the Lord of the Worlds. (Qur'an 7:54)

These verses remind us that nothing can come to life on its own. Everything, including the earth we live on and the heavens we see above, was created by Almighty God.

God does not merely create and abandon His creatures. He goes on fashioning and evolving new forms. He sustains all that He has created according to His ways. "He is Allah, the Creator, the Shaper out of naughts, the Fashioner. His are the most beautiful names" (Qur'an 59:24). He is the Sustainer of the universe.

God has created man and kindly provided for him. Concerning the creation of man, the Qur'an says,

> He it is Who created you from dust, then from a drop (of seed) then from a clot, then bringeth you forth as a child, then (ordaineth) that ye attain full strength and afterward that ye become old men—though some among you die before—and that ye reach an appointed term, that haply ye may understand (Qur'an 40:67-68).

God created all that we can see and cannot see, by the divine command "Be." And "there it was." By this very command, the Lord created the universe and all that is in it.

It is the sincere Muslim belief that God did not rest after creating the universe and all the creatures. He needs no rest like humans and animals. God is absolute life, which is free from any such need. The Qur'an says, "There is no God save Him, the Alive, the Eternal. Neither slumber nor sleep overtaketh Him. Unto Him belongeth whatsoever is in the heavens and whatsoever is in the earth" (Qur'an 2:255). God is active as the Creator, the Life Giver and Life Remover, the Sustainer and the sole Controller of all His creation.

The names of God
God is the Supreme Reality. He has revealed to humankind ninety-nine beautiful names *(al-asma al husna)* which indicate His transcendent majesty and unity. The Qur'an says, "Allah's are the fairest names. Invoke Him by them. And leave the company of those who blaspheme His names. They will be requited what they do" (Qur'an 7:180).

In a *Hadith*[2] reported by Abu Huraira, the Prophet (Peace be upon him) [PBUH] is reported to have said, "Verily there are ninety-nine names of Allah, and whosoever recites them shall enter Paradise." [3]

These names are not used to divide Allah, for Allah cannot be more than One, but rather to express some of His attributes. Muslims use these names in reverence for God and as part of praise and prayer. God may always be invoked by a name relevant to the need of His beseecher. We shall be describing some of these names, such as *Rahman* (most Gracious), *Rahim* (most Merciful), or *al-Fialil* (most Majestic).

God is merciful

All surahs of the Qur'an except one[4] begin with the *Basmalah*[5]—the statement, "In the Name of Allah, the Compassionate (or Beneficent), the Merciful." The Basmalah is the common statement a Muslim must recite before doing anything. It constantly reminds the believer of the mercy of God to all His creation. A careful look at the Qur'an shows that there are numerous *ayat* (verses) which describe God's love and mercy for mankind.

Allah says in the Holy Qur'an, "Allah it is Who hath appointed for you night that ye may rest therein, and day for seeing. Lo! Allah is a Lord of bounty for mankind, yet most of mankind give not thanks" (Qur'an 40:61).

God continues in another verse,

Allah it is Who appointed for you *the earth for a dwelling place* and the sky for a canopy, and fashioned you and perfected your shapes, and hath provided you with good things. Such is Allah, your Lord. Then blessed be Allah, the Lord of the Worlds.

(Qur'an 40:64)

Humans enjoy the mercy of God Who is kind and good. God's mercy is to anyone, believer or unbeliever, obedient or disobedient, Muslim or non-Muslim, black or white.

The Qur'an states, "Allah is He Who created the heavens and the earth, and causeth water to descend from the sky, thereby producing fruits as food for you" (Qur'an 14:32). The Qur'an continues, "And He giveth you of all ye ask of Him, and if ye would count the bounty of Allah he cannot reckon it. Lo! man is verily a wrong-doer, an ingrate" (Qur'an 14:34).

God's mercy for His creation is immeasurable. We cannot imagine or count His favors to humankind. He gives people food, drink, the means of movement, and all the necessities of life. He provides for them irrespective of their behavior. God has created humans in the best form of creation and has given them everything they need for spiritual and physical growth. God has given all this because of His mercy. God is the all-Merciful, and through His mercy persons attain peace, tranquility, hope, and confidence. The mercy of God is real and active; it pervades all the dimensions of the human experience.

Furthermore, God has promised to extend His love to those who obey His will. His mercy is extended to all humankind. His love is extended to those who submit to His will. The Qur'an says, "Say, (O Muhammad, to mankind) If ye love Allah, follow me; Allah will love you and forgive you your sins. Allah is Forgiving, Merciful" (Qur'an 3:31).

God is all-powerful

Having seen that God is Compassionate and Merciful, we must also note that it is only God Who possesses all power. None besides Allah can benefit or harm a person. Only God can provide for human needs or give and take away life. The Holy Qur'an proclaims, "Knowest thou not that it is Allah unto Whom belongeth the sovereignty of the heavens and earth; and ye have not, beside Allah, any friend or helper" (Qur'an 2:107). With God alone rests the authority to exercise power in the heavens, on earth, and over the entire creation.

God's supreme authority and power cannot be challenged by anyone or anything. He is the Supreme Master of the whole universe as well as its Creator. A Qur'anic verse which comments on God's sovereign power reads,

Say, O Allah! Owner of Sovereignty! Thou givest sovereignty unto whom Thou wilt, and Thou withdrawest sovereignty from whom Thou wilt. Thou exaltest whom Thou wilt and Thou abasest whom Thou wilt. In Thy hand is the good. Lo! Thou art Able to do all things. (Qur'an 3:26)

This is a serious admonition from Allah to those who hold power on earth. They should remember that God gives power and also removes rulers from power as He pleases. He is capable of doing this because all power comes from Him; He is the Lord of power.

"Now Allah be exalted, the True King! There is no God save Him, the Lord of the Throne of Grace. He who crieth unto any other god along with Allah hath no proof thereof" (Qur'an 23:116-117). This verse explains the nature of the power of God. He is the most exalted Power, the Sovereign, the Master. The firm belief in the all-powerful nature of God can help man to give the best possible explanation of many mysterious things that happen in life.

Allah is the undisputed Authority Who alone is entitled to receive obedience, and in fact receives it. He is the most Supreme, so heads should bow to Him in submission and adoration. Powerful as He is, God remains pure and free from all sins and evil.

God is wise and all-knowing

The Omnipotent, Merciful, Benevolent Allah is also all-wise and all-knowing (omniscient). The Holy Qur'an teaches, "And keep your opinion secret or proclaim it, lo! He is Knower of all that is in the breasts (of persons). Should He not know what He created? And He is the Subtle, the Aware" (Qur'an 67:13-14).

Muslims take these attributes of God's knowledge very seriously. For instance, one should not commit sins in the dark thinking that because there is no one around one is not being noticed. God's knowledge extends to everything seen or unseen, spoken or unspoken. Nothing is hidden from Him, desires or undeclared intentions.

God's wisdom and knowledge is stressed in several verses of the Qur'an. For instance, He says,

His is the praise in the Hereafter, and He is the Wise, the Aware. . . . Not an atom's weight, or less than that or greater escapeth Him in the heavens or in the earth, but it is a clear record. (Qur'an 34:1, 3)

And He knoweth what is in the land and the sea. Not a leaf falleth but He knoweth it, not a grain amid the darkness of the earth, naught of wet or dry but [it is noted] in a clear record. (Qur'an 6:59)

It is the perfect God Who knows everything happening in the present and in the future. He knows what is near and far, what is in heaven and on earth. His knowledge is unbound. He instructs humans in wisdom through His messengers and written Scriptures. He also reveals to humans the knowledge of the laws of nature and His wonderful signs in His creation and in the order of the universe. This is all part of His wisdom and knowledge.

God is eternal
As Muslims we are strongly commanded to believe and know that God is eternal. By this we acknowledge that God has no beginning and no end, that He has been there and will be there always. There is none after Him nor before Him. He was when there was nothing and will be when there will be nothing. The Qur'an states, "He is the First and the Last, and the Outward and the Inward; and He is Knower of all things" (Qur'an 57:3).

The eternal God is not limited by time, space, place, or circumstance. As He exists beyond time, He cannot go into senility. God is preexistent and eternal, yet other forms of existence will come to an end. Everything that exists will perish except God Who will endure forever. The Qur'an teaches, "Everyone that is thereon will pass away; There remaineth but the countenance of thy Lord of Might and Glory" (Qur'an 55:26-27). This teaching is important because it reminds the believers that as human beings we are nothing but visitors on this world. God alone is eternally living and present; all else is transient.

The most magnificent human works, such as spacecraft or skyscrapers, are nothing in the eyes of God. The great empires, the marvelous works of science, art, and all other spheres of human endeavor will perish. The great wonders of nature such as the mountains, the valleys, the seas, the stars, the sun, and the moon will equally perish at the time God wills. Only God the Supreme Master of the whole universe and the Creator of everything will remain.

Summary
In attempting to understand the nature and works of God, we learn God is only One without partner or son. He is Creator of the

universe and everything found in it. He is the Compassionate and Merciful and His mercy is to all creatures. He is just. He is the Guide and Guardian of everything. He is preexistent and eternal. He is all-knowing and all-wise. He is loving and provident, and His mercy for His creatures knows no boundary. He is holy and cannot commit sins or do evil. He is independent and unique.

Because He is unique, people cannot know everything about God, and even the list of ninety-nine names of God is not in any way exhaustive. Nevertheless, the Muslim can acknowledge God through reflection, meditation, firm commitment to the credal statement, *La ilaha illa 'llah,* and the total peaceful surrender to His commands and will.

A CHRISTIAN RESPONSE

Christians and Muslims worship the same God. Both give witness that there is One true and only God, the righteous and transcendent Creator of all things in heaven and earth. Furthermore, Christians accept with thankfulness all ninety-nine names of God that Muslims repeat in worship and praise to God. Even the name Allah is affirmed by Christians as a name of God. The Prophet Abraham knew God as El or Elohim, which is a Hebrew form of the Arabic *Allah.* It is no wonder the Qur'an affirms that those closest to the Muslims are the Christians. The profound Muslim appreciation of the sovereignty and transcendence of God is a witness Christians need to hear.

Nevertheless, within our common faith in God, Muslims and Christians experience differences. These differences are rooted in different understandings of God's relationship to people. The Qur'an stresses the revelation of God's commands and His names to humans. In the Bible we perceive God as the One Who reveals Himself to humankind.

The biblical witness is that God has chosen to reveal Himself in personal self-disclosure with humankind. God as the One Who encounters personally is known as Yahweh, the covenant God, the "I AM," Who is always present calling people into a covenant relationship with Himself. Yahweh reveals not only His will, commands, and names to humankind, but also Himself in personal self-disclosure.

The Bible reveals that Yahweh in His self-disclosure reveals that He is the One Who loves us perfectly. In fact, the biblical witness is that Yahweh God gives Himself in suffering, redemptive love. Because of His love, He sorrows when we sorrow, He suffers when we suffer, He is pained by our sin. God loves us totally.

The Christian witness is that God invites us into a covenant fellowship with Himself; God invites us to know and have fellowship with the One Whom Islam praises through the reverent repetition of His ninety-nine glorious names.

Notes

1. The word *Allah* is Arabic and difficult to translate exactly. The word means the unique God Who possesses all the attributes of perfection and beauty in their infinitude. Muslims feel strongly that the English word *God* does not convey the real meaning of the word *Allah*. However, in this book *Allah* and *God* will be used interchangeably.

2. *Hadith* means prophetic tradition.

3. Reported by Abu Huraira, *Sahih Muslim*, Vol. IV (Lahore: M. Ashraf-by Siddiqi, 1975), p. 1409.

4. Surat Tauba (chapter 9).

5. In Arabic transliteration the Basmalah reads, *Bis-mi-llahi ar-Rahmani ar-Rahim.*

In the Name of Allah, the Compassionate, the Merciful.

2
The Creation

THE MUSLIM VIEW

'Lo! your Lord is Allah Who created the heavens and the earth in six days'[1] (Qur'an 7:54). The Holy Qur'an and the Traditions (Hadith) of the Holy Prophet (PBUH) describe the Muslim attitude of praise to Allah for the marvel of creation.

We have already explained how God is Creator of the universe and all living and nonliving things to be found therein. Our major concern in this chapter will be to examine the relationship between humankind, nature, and God, the Creator of all.

The earth and universe were created by God through a long step-by-step process. The Qur'an describes the basic process of the formation of the universe in this way:

> Have not those who disbelieve known that the heavens and the earth were of one piece, then We parted them, and We made every living thing of water? Will they not then believe? And We have placed in the earth firm hills lest it quake with them, and we have placed therein ravines as roads that haply they may find their way. And we have made the sky a roof withheld (from them). Yet they turn away from its portents. And He it is Who created the night and the day, and the sun and the moon. They float, each in an orbit. (Qur'an 21:30-33)

These verses of the Qur'an indicate the evolution of the ordered world. The Qur'anic witness further testifies that God created the heavens and earth and what is between them in six "periods," and no weariness touched Him (Qur'an 50:38). God created the universe and the earth in an orderly step-by-step progression.

We also learn that all life began in water, a view which is complemented by modern science. The Qur'an further testifies to Allah's ordering the earth:

> And He made dark the night thereof, and He brought forth the morn thereof. And after that He spread the earth. And produced therefrom the water thereof and the pasture thereof, And He made fast the hills, A provision for you and for your cattle. (Qur'an 79:29-33)

We can deduce from the Qur'anic witness that not only is God the Creator of the whole universe, but that He has also created it in an orderly and understandable manner. Probably people are last in God's creation process. God has created things in the heavens,[2] things on earth, things between the heavens and the earth, and things beneath the soil. "Unto Him belongeth whatsoever is in the heavens and whatsoever is in the earth, and whatsoever is between them, and whatsoever is beneath the sod" (Qur'an 20:6).

In summary, the Qur'anic witness on creation is as follows: First, there were six periods for the creation in general. Second, there was an interlocking of the stages in the creation of the heavens and the earth. Third, the universe was initially a unique mass all in one block, which God by His power and will split up. Fourth, there is a plurality of heavens and earth, seven heavens being emphasized. Fifth, there is an intermediary world of planets and heavenly bodies between the heavens and the earth. Sixth, God alone is the Creator of nature and the universe, and neither of the two can be God or be worshiped as such, for God is altogether transcendent over creation. Seventh, and finally, God created everything in an orderly and understandable manner.

Man as khalifa

It is appropriate to ask ourselves, What role has God given humans as far as His creation is concerned? We have already said that humankind was part of creation and possibly the last being whom God created. Humans were created in a special way. The Lord of the universe bestowed upon them the faculties of learning, speaking, understanding, and discerning the right from the wrong and good from evil. Since they alone possess these qualities, they enjoy a specially high status in the hierarchy of all known creatures, both in heaven and on earth.

The first man God created was Adam. He was the first human being to appear either in heaven or on earth. Adam was created as a *khalifa* (vicegerent) of God on earth. According to the Holy Qur'an, the Lord said to the angels:

> And when thy Lord said unto the angels: Lo! I am about to place a viceroy in the earth, they said: Wilt Thou place therein one who will do harm therein and will shed blood, while we, hymn Thy praise and sanctify Thee? He said: Surely I know that which ye know not. (Qur'an 2:30)

After this God created Adam from clay, and he was taught the names of all things and the knowledge of their properties (Qur'an 2:31). God then set these things before the angels and asked them, "Inform me of the names of these, if ye are truthful" (Qur'an 2:31).

Although Adam had been taught the names of all things in the presence of the angels, they could not recall a single name so they replied, "Be glorified! We have no knowledge saving that which Thou hast taught us. Lo! Thou, only Thou, art the Knower, the Wise" (Qur'an 2:32).

Then God asked Adam to tell the angels all the names of the things taught to him. Adam related correctly all the names as taught, much to the surprise of the angels. So God declared the knowledge of His khalifa on earth as superior to that of His angels. He ordered all His angels to bow down to Adam; all obeyed except *Iblis* (Satan) who proudly refused and hence rejected the faith. (See Qur'an 2:34.)

About this time God created a mate (wife) for Adam to give him company. Her name was Hauwa (Eve). The Qur'an states,

> And We said: O Adam! Dwell thou and thy wife in the Garden, and eat ye freely (of the fruits) thereof where ye will; but come not nigh this tree lest ye become wrongdoers. (Qur'an 2:35)

We have observed that Allah created humans in a special way and gave them special status. Adam was to be the khalifa of God. Then God taught him the names of all creatures, which he learned perfectly. God then asked the angels to prostrate themselves before man, which all except Satan did.[3] What does all this mean? It means that God gave man the possibility of having control over all things, for to possess the name of a thing would mean to exercise power over it. The Qur'an says: "Lo! the earth is Allah's. He giveth it for an inheritance to whom He will" (Qur'an 7:128).

God has honored man, His khalifa, with the authority over His countless creatures. Humans have been commissioned to use nature for their own welfare (Qur'an 33:72). As a khalifa, humans are chosen to cultivate the land and enrich life with knowledge and meaning. Nature is subject to humans. The superior position man holds in the eyes of God makes man an authority over all God's creation. Humans alone enjoy the right to use nature for their own good in obedience to the Divine commands.

The Qur'an teaches,

> Allah it is Who hath made the sea of service unto you that the ships may run thereon by His command. . . . And hath made of service unto you whatsoever is in the heavens and whatsoever is in the earth. (Qur'an 45:12-13)

The sea mentioned here is but one example of Allah's wonderful care in making all things in nature available for the service of humans. While subduing nature for their own good, people should remember that it is all from God. They are only God's khalifa on earth. They should therefore use nature responsibly in obedience to the revealed commands of God.

The rights of nature

Although the superior position of humans gives them authority over God's creation, they sometimes overstep their limits. Islam teaches that all creation has certain rights that cannot be violated by humankind. This means that humans are not free to misuse nature. The fundamental right of God's creation (nature) is that it should not be wasted on fruitless ventures, nor should it be unnecessarily hurt, harmed, or destroyed. For instance, Islam disapproves of the useless cutting of trees and bushes. The khalifa can use the fruits and other produce of the forests or grasslands, but has no right wantonly to destroy them. After all, plants and vegetables have life. "And We send down from the sky blessed water whereby we give growth unto gardens and the grain of crops. . . . Provision (made) for men" (Qur'an 50:9-11).

The khalifa is free to explore the planets above the earth but has no right to attempt destroying them. Islam prohibits the waste of even lifeless things. It even disapproves of the wasteful flow of water; it recommends only a limited and prescribed quantity which one should use for *wadu* (ablution) and *ghusul* (a complete bath).

Even for food, Allah does not permit wastage or excess. It is wrong to overeat when others are hungry. Muslims are allowed to slaughter animals for food, but have been prohibited from killing them for fun, sport, or naughtiness. And when an animal is slaughtered, it should be done with the least possible degree of pain. The name of the Life Giver is besought before slaughter, as a reminder that life must not be taken away thoughtlessly but rather for the purpose of food. Hunting is allowed only if it is for food. However, dangerous and venomous animals may be killed because human life is more precious than that of dangerous animals. Again, they should be killed with the least possible degree of pain. Beasts of burden must be treated kindly and humanely. Birds should not be caged unless there is a very good reason for doing so.

Summary
In summary, we have seen that God, the Creator of all, has taught humankind to use nature but avoid the waste and destruction of nature in every way. Nature is the provision of the merciful Allah for the sustenance of humans; they are therefore commanded to make the best use of God's created resources on earth. Responsible stewardship in obedience to God's Divine commands is the key to the Muslim approach to development.

A CHRISTIAN RESPONSE
Islam and Christianity both recognize that nature is a wonderful creation of God. Humans are called by God to use nature with

thankfulness and responsibility. The destruction and selfish exploitation of nature is condemned by both Christians and Muslims. Christians identify deeply with the Muslim appreciation of nature as God's good and wonderful creation. They both also recognize their dependence on God in using nature responsibly.

Nevertheless, there seem to be some differences also between the Muslim and Christian understanding of nature. For example, in Islam we learn that God taught man the names of all things; in the biblical account we read that man was commanded to name the animals. In Islam humankind is the khalifa of God on earth; in Christianity humans are commanded to have dominion over the earth. Does this suggest that in the biblical account people are given considerable personal freedom, authority, and responsibility to use nature for their own good ?

However, the Bible does warn that persons live most joyously in their relationships to nature when they are also living in a right and joyous relationship with God.

The purpose of the Bible is to reveal the meaning of life; it is not a book of scientific information. Part of biblical revelation shows that the earth is God's good and orderly creation. Beyond that the Bible does not go. It is humankind's own responsibility to understand how God put the earth together, to probe the mysteries of the laws of nature. In the Bible we read that God commanded man to "subdue," "fill," "till," "rule," "take care of" the earth.

Notes

1. Muslim commentators on the Qur'an feel the six days represent a metaphorical period. A day in the sight of God can range from 1000 to 50,000 years of our reckoning (see Qur'an 70:4). These days of creation are in fact long periods numbering six.

2. Muslims believe God has created seven heavens: "Allah it is Who hath created seven heavens" (Qur'an 65:12).

3. Muslim theology is of the view that *Iblis* (Satan) was not an angel but a *jinn* (spirit) and that he was a leader of a group of jinns who disobeyed Allah.

In the Name of Allah, the Compassionate, the Merciful.

3
Adam and Hauwa

THE MUSLIM BELIEF

"I have made him and have breathed into him of My spirit" (Qur'an 15:29). In another Qur'anic verse Allah says: "Thy Lord said unto the angels: Lo! I am about to place a (khalifa) in the earth" (Qur'an 2:30). Muslim scholars are not fully agreed what the meaning is of man as the khalifa (vicegerent) of God, or of receiving the spirit of God. Some modern Muslim scholars believe that the Qur'anic evidence suggests that man has a certain Godlikeness. But the orthodox belief is that man has no Godlikeness. God breathing into man His (God's) spirit is explained by some scholars as the faculty of Godlike knowledge and will, which if rightly used gives man superiority over all creation. However, this is not to make God into man, for God is absolutely transcendent.

Nevertheless, man is a dignified, honorable being who has been infused with God's spirit, and has been commissioned to be His khalifa on earth. Man enjoys the office of khalifa, because he alone of all God's creatures is gifted with the rational faculties, spiritual aspirations, and the powers of conscious action. The Lord of the universe and its Master has created the earth and has entrusted man to be the caretaker. Allah has granted man a limited autonomy, appointed him as His khalifa on earth, and has firmly instructed him to live according to His guidance.

As God has breathed into man His spirit there is, therefore, something in man which is special, something that man was at least bound to retain in some proportion. That special thing is:

(a) the intelligence (or knowledge) to discern between right and wrong, good and evil, reality and illusion.

(b) the will to choose freely between good and bad, true and false, right and evil.

(c) the authority to acquire and make use of things around him.

(d) The power of speech—to be able to express his worship of his Creator.

All the above are spiritual qualities which God has entrusted to man, and if rightly used they enable man to submit to the will of Allah. We further note that when God created man, He instructed man to worship Him, and none else. He placed man on earth for a fixed time as a test of the manner in which man would use the special spiritual qualities which God has given. God created man to worship Him, and not to be His equal or rival in any way. So the spiritual qualities of man are proportionate to his finite nature.

Good as man may be, he still cannot measure up to the goodness and perfection of Allah, his Creator. History has shown that man is negligent, careless, and forgetful. He is good but imperfect. Being imperfect, he needs constant reminding. That is why God sent His prophets and messengers to help man achieve perfection. Through the prophets, God has repeatedly reminded man of the Law of God.

The first Muslims
It is the Muslim witness that Adam, Allah's first khalifa on earth and the first man in creation, was also the first Prophet sent for the guidance of mankind. Prophecy begins with the first man. The first man on earth is given clear guidance and a law to follow and to pass on to his descendants. This law was and still is "Islam," submission to Allah.

It is the sincere Muslim witness that the first phase of life on earth did not begin in sin and rebellion against the Creator. Although Adam and Hauwa (Eve) were sent from the Heavenly Garden down to earth after Satan's temptation,[1] they realized their sin and repented. They sought forgiveness from God. They were given the necessary guidance. Adam was a true Prophet of Allah. They were the first true Muslims.

This is clearly revealed in the Qur'an. We read, "They said: 'Our Lord! We have wronged ourselves. If Thou forgive us not and have not mercy on us, surely we are of the lost' " (Qur'an 7:23). The merciful Allah sent them down to earth with the words, "And We said: 'Fall down, one of you a foe unto the other! There shall be for you on earth a habitation and provision for a time' " (Qur'an 2:36).

Nevertheless man's presence on earth is not a punishment, but rather a test of his commitment to the will of Allah. Although He sent them to earth after Satan's temptation, He certainly forgave them. The Qur'an says, "Then Adam received from his Lord words (of salvation), and He relented toward him. Lo! He is the Relenting, the Merciful" (Qur'an 2 :37).

Because God is all-loving and all-merciful, in spite of man's mistakes, God assured him of guidance. He said, "Go down, all of you, from hence; but verily there cometh unto you from Me a guidance; and whosofolloweth My guidance, there shall no fear come on them neither shall they grieve" (Qur'an 2:38).

So the first man was given both inspiration and guidance for the whole of mankind. God assures man that anybody who follows this guidance will be free from any fear for the present or the future and any grief for the past.

Many Muslims think that Adam and Hauwa were first kept in the Heavenly Garden for a trial of their inclinations before they were to be sent to the earth where they had been appointed as khalifa.[2] The Garden was the most suitable place for the test because it was actually Paradise (*Janna*). Man was shown that Paradise was the suitable place for him to live, but if he yielded to Satan's temptations he could not remain in Paradise. The only way to regain the "Garden" was to oppose Satan relentlessly and successfully by obeying the Law of God. The Prophet Adam received true guidance so that he himself and his family and descendants could submit to Allah's will as obedient Muslims, and thereby regain Paradise.

It is significant that Hauwa (Eve) was just as responsible for yielding to Satan as was Adam. They were both tempted, they both repented, and they were both blessed and forgiven by the merciful Allah. Both were true Muslims. So woman and man are equal in the sight of God. They are both God's khalifa on earth. No Muslim should attribute the first mistake to the woman. In Islam woman is not inferior to man, nor man inferior to woman.

The frailty of humanity

All people are born as true Muslims, innocent, pure, and free (Qur'an 30:30). No single act which has warped the human will. Any concept of original sin is contrary to the true teachings of Islam. It is not a sin for man to be fallible. As a finite creature, he is bound to be imperfect. However, it becomes a sin if man has the means of perfection and decides not to avail himself of them. Man is not responsible for committing any childhood sin. He only becomes responsible after he grows up, is given intellect by God, and is able to distinguish between right and wrong. This is the only time when he can bear responsibility for his actions before his Creator. Nevertheless, because man is born good, what he becomes after birth is largely the result of external influence and environment.

Although man is a good and responsible being, committing sinful acts is the responsibility of the actual offender. According to Muslim witness, sin is not hereditary, for no man is born a sinner. Similarly sin is not communal in nature nor is it transferable. God has given man freedom of will, and man is therefore personally responsible for his own actions, good or bad, right or wrong. A man can misuse his freedom and fall into corruption and all other vices, but at the same time he is capable of reform and can be forgiven if he sincerely chooses to submit to God's guidance. Sin is acquirable, but not innate, and therefore, if man rightly uses those special qualities which he has been endowed with, he can easily avoid sin. Sin is not inevitable, because man is not sinful.

Summary

In conclusion, the Muslim view of man can be summarized thus: Man is a dignified, honorable creature, into whom God has breathed his spirit. This spirit can be referred to as Godlike knowledge and will; it does not suggest that man is the likeness of God, the equal of God, or the rival of God. The spiritual qualities man has received are only proportionate to his finite nature. Man has also been made God's khalifa on earth.

Islam does not believe that humanity is sinful. Rather Islam teaches that man is not perfect. Only God is perfect! But imperfect man forgets and is negligent. For this reason man has to be reminded constantly of the right path through Prophets and revelation.

A CHRISTIAN RESPONSE

What is man? That is the question. What does it mean for humans to receive the Spirit of God? Certainly it means that persons are the highest creation, as Islam testifies. The Bible says that humankind is a little lower than the angels, but crowned with glory and honor (Heb. 2:7).

The Christian witness enlarges on the Islamic belief that humankind received the Spirit of God when created. The Bible says, "Then the Lord God formed man of the dust from the ground, and breathed into his nostrils the breath of life; and man became a living being" (Gen. 2:7). It also says, "So God created man in his own image, in the image of God he created him, male and female he created them" (Gen. 1:27). To say that humans are created in the image of God does not mean that God looks like them or that they look like God. It does mean that humans have profound Godlike qualities. This Godlikeness means especially that people have the capability of fellowship with God. People can know God. They are capable of enjoying a covenant fellowship with their Creator; they are personal; they are Godlike.

Islam emphasizes human intellectual capabilities. The Christian faith is especially impressed by humans as covenant or fellowship creatures. In Islam humankind is created for obedience to the will of God. Christians believe that humans finds their fullest humanity in joyous communion with God and other persons.

The Bible also describes what happens when people turn from God. When people rebel against God, they become evil and sinful. Christians believe that the image of God in which they were created is spoiled whenever they do not live in a right and joyous relationship with God. The Bible says, "All have sinned and fall short of the glory of God" (Rom. 3:23).

A MUSLIM CLARIFICATION

It is doubtful whether the spirit of God which Adam received according to Islam is the same as the Christian understanding of the Spirit of God. As mentioned above, Muslims believe the spirit refers to life which comes from God and which has endowed man with qualities which are superior to other creatures, most notably, superior intelligence, will, authority, and speech.

Notes

1. Satan was also expelled from heaven.

2. A. Maududi, *The Meaning of the Qur'an,* Vol. I (Lahore: Islamic Publications Ltd., 1971), pp. 58-59.

In the Name of Allah, the Compassionate, the Merciful.

4
Satan and Evil

THE SOURCE OF EVIL

It is our sincere belief as Muslims that Satan (Iblis) has been the source and center of evil since even before the creation of Adam, the first human in history. Satan was the first creature to disobey and lead a rebellion against God, long before the creation of man. The Holy Qur'an relates,

> And (remember) when thy Lord said unto the angels: Lo! I am creating a mortal out of potter's clay of black mud altered, so, when I have made him and have breathed into him of My spirit, do ye fall down, prostrating yourselves unto him. So the angels fell prostrate, all of them together save Iblis. He refused to be among the prostrate (Qur'an 15:28-31).[1]

This disobedience of Iblis was the source and origin of evil among mankind. When God asked Iblis why he refused to prostrate, he replied, "Why should I prostrate myself unto a mortal whom Thou hast created out of potter's clay of black mud altered (Qur'an 15:33)? He added that he was far better than man because he was created out of fire (or light). Man was created out of clay.

When God created the first man, infused His spirit into him, appointed him to be His khalifa, gave him the names of all things, tested the angels on the same names and they failed, and ordered all the angels to prostrate to Adam, Iblis proudly refused. Iblis became an unbeliever. He is, therefore, the source of evil.

Iblis was proud that he had been made out of light and therefore was much better than man made out of clay. What Iblis had missed was that man, though created out of clay, had been created in the best form, had received part of God's spirit, and had been made a khalifa of God. None of these honors had ever been bestowed to any other creature, either in heaven or on earth. We see that arrogance, egoism, jealousy, and rebellion, which are the very sources of evil, were (and are) the exclusive possession of Satan.

Because Iblis proudly refused to bow down to man, and even abused the angels who prostrated themselves as well as the man to whom they bowed, God rejected and cursed him. God said, "Then go thou forth from hence, for verily thou art outcast. And lo! the curse shall be on thee till the Days of Judgment" (Qur'an 15:34-35). Despite the rejection, Iblis put in one more request, which was subsequently granted. He said, "My Lord! Reprieve me till the day when they are raised" (Qur'an 15:36). The reprieve (respite) was granted to Iblis until the appointed day. Again the same evil Iblis proposed to God thus:

He said: My Lord! Because Thou has sent me astray, I verily shall adorn the path of error for them in the earth, and shall mislead them everyone. Save such of them as are Thy perfectly devoted slaves. (Qur'an 15:39-40)

Allah replied to the wicked Iblis, who even falsely blamed God for his evil ways:

This is a right course incumbent on Me: Lo! as for My slaves, thou has not power over any of them save such of the froward as follow thee, and lo! for all such, hell will be the promised place. It hath seven gates, and each gate hath an appointment portion. Lo! those who ward off (evil) are among gardens and watersprings. (And it is said unto them): Enter them in peace, secure. (Qur'an 15:41-46)

From this discussion, we learn that Iblis has been the arch enemy of humankind from the time of creation to the present (Qur'an 7:14-18). Satan started his evil activities on the first man whom God had created. He has continued his evil seductions ever since.

After God had cursed Iblis, He said to Adam, "Dwell thou and thy wife in the Garden and eat from whence ye will, but come not nigh this tree lest ye become wrong-doers" (Qur'an 7:19).

At this time our first parents, Adam and Hauwa, were quite innocent in spiritual and material affairs. They had been placed in a spiritual Garden of innocence and bliss which was not on the earth but in the heavens. They did not know evil. However, as God's khalifa, they had been endowed, through the spirit of God, with the faculties of knowledge, will, and choice. Although they had the capacity to do wrong, they needed to choose to reject evil. God, Who is all-knowing and all-wise, decided to test his khalifa by giving them a choice, a small prohibition. In this beautiful Garden humans were prohibited from approaching only one tree—the forbidden tree. But they succumbed to the temptations of the Master of Evil.

About this event, the Qur'an says,

> Then Satan whispered to them that he might manifest unto them that which was hidden from them of their shame, and he said: Your Lord forbade you from this tree only lest ye should become angels or become of the immortals. And he swore unto them (saying): Lo! I am a sincere adviser unto you (Qur'an 7:20-21).

So, by deceit, Iblis seduced Adam and his wife, Hauwa, to eat from the tree, hence bringing about their fall from the Garden to earth. What was more dramatic is that when they ate, their shame became visible to them for the first time. They hurriedly covered themselves with leaves from the Garden. Soon their Lord called to them saying, "Did I not forbid you from that tree and tell you: Lo! Satan is an open enemy to you?" (Qur'an 7:22). Thus the chief of evil managed to swerve the progenitors of humankind from the straight path, away from the will of their Lord.

We must also consider that Adam and Hauwa ate the fruit of the forbidden tree as a result of Satan's deceit and temptation. Of course they disobeyed God and thus committed a sin, but at the same time we must realize that actually it was not a willful and deliberate disobedience. Again we note that when God called on them, they quickly realized their sinfulness. They prayed to Him to forgive them. They did not turn away from God. They said, "Our Lord! We have wronged ourselves. If thou forgive us not and have not mercy on us, surely we are of the lost!" (Qur'an 7:23).

Adam and Hauwa had felt shame, guilt, and remorse for their disobedience toward Allah. They lost the joyful state of the Garden. That is why they prayed for God's mercy. As Muslims we can deduce from this event that man is imperfect, even if he lives in heaven. At the same time we learn that committing a sin of the gravity of Adam and Hauwa's does not deter the human heart from spiritual reform.

Humans as God's khalifa have been endowed with sufficient knowledge to enable them to realize their sins and pitfalls. Better still, this knowledge helps them to know where and to whom to turn for guidance. Islamic witness is that Allah is always ready through His mercy and grace to forgive the sins of all who sincerely seek His guidance and make up their minds to change for the better. The worst sin in Islam is *shirk* (associating Allah with other gods). But even the atheists, polytheists, or pantheists can be forgiven by Allah if they confess their sins before Allah and sincerely submit to His commands and will.

When Adam and Hauwa prayed for Allah's mercy and forgiveness, they even lacked the correct words of expression, but Allah, Who is all-merciful and most forgiving, taught Adam and Hauwa the prayer for seeking repentance. Allah pardoned them as the Qur'an witnesses: "Then Adam received from his Lord words (of revelation), and He relented toward him. Lo! He is the Relenting, the Merciful" (Qur'an 2:37). Adam and Hauwa were thus absolved of the sin of disobedience, and their future descendants were made immune from its effect. Allah did not only accept Adam's repentance but went ahead and appointed him as His messenger to give guidance to humankind.

Nevertheless, after Allah had pardoned Adam and Hauwa, He sent them down to earth from the Heavenly Garden. The expulsion from Paradise included Iblis, the bitter enemy of man. This is shown in the phrase "enemies to each other" (Qur'an 7 :24), which means that God decreed that Iblis and man shall be adversaries of one another. Iblis tries his most to divert man from the path of God into the path of evil. But man is commanded, through divine guidance, to fight Iblis as his number one enemy. Islam further observes that the evil touches only those who yield to it, and it has no power over Allah's sincere servants who have been forgiven because of His mercy.

So, in Islam, evil is avoidable if one is sincere in one's worship of Allah. It is forgivable if the sinner confesses to Allah. It is not hereditary.

Summary

The Muslim witness is that Iblis, who disobeyed Allah even before the creation of man, is the source of evil. Although the first man Adam and his wife, Hauwa, sinned, it was not a deliberate desire to disobey their Creator. They were tempted by the master of evil—Iblis. They sincerely confessed to Allah, Who granted them pardon. Humankind does not suffer sin and evil because of Adam's disobedience. Sin is not hereditary. Adam, having repented, was made Allah's first messenger on earth. He was to show guidance to his children. How could God entrust such a high office to an evildoer?

A CHRISTIAN RESPONSE

The Christian witness is that the origin of evil is the misuse of personal freedom. Satan misused his freedom. He rebelled against God and subsequently became exceedingly evil. Multitudes of angels and spirits have followed his example. The biblical witness is that Satan tempted humans to sin, and they have also decided to yield to Satan's temptation. Adam and Eve chose to disobey God. They took the fruit which God had forbidden. They ran from God and hid in the bushes. They decided to turn away from God (Gen. 3:1-24).

The decision of humankind to turn away from God is the root of evil. In our disobedience we become evil. The image of God in which we are created is tragically spoiled because we have collectively and individually turned away from God. God is not to be blamed. We ourselves have turned away from God. For this reason we experience guilt and death. The Bible says, "For the wages of sin is death" (Rom. 6:23).

Notes

1. See also Qur'an 7:11, 2:34.

In the Name of Allah, the Compassionate, the Merciful.

5
The Books of God

WHAT ARE THE MUSLIM SCRIPTURES?

Adam was the first person to receive guidance from God. After he had shown sorrow for his sin (as discussed in the previous chapter), he was forgiven. At the same time God promised to give Adam guidance. He sent Adam to earth to serve as God's khalifa and appointed Adam His first messenger to give guidance to his children and the rest of humankind.

No sooner were Adam and his children settled on earth than Satan started playing his evil tricks again. But whenever chaos, confusion, or evil filled human society, God sent a message for the reform of society. This message was often contained in the Holy Books (Scriptures), which were revealed to His prophets and messengers. However, not all prophets and messengers were given Holy Books. God revealed His Divine Books only to some prophets and messengers.

As Muslims it is a central part of our faith to believe in the four Holy Books (Scriptures) of Allah. All of these four Books are holy and originate from God. They are inscribed on eternal tablets in heaven. Exact copies of these Divine, heavenly Scriptures have been sent down from God (*tanzil*) from time to time. These revealed Scriptures consist of four Books. They have much in common and all four Books have the same purpose: to reform humankind. They confirm one another. Muslims are required to accept and believe in them completely. There is also a fifth Book of God, which as you will note in the following list, is not available, for it has been lost.

The books are:

The *Suhuf* (Scrolls) These are ten Holy Scriptures revealed to the

Prophet Ibrahim (Abraham) (PBUH), but unfortunately they are now extinct and not traceable in existing world literature.

The *Taurat* (Torah) This was a Holy Book revealed to the Prophet Musa (Moses) (PBUH).

The *Zabur* (Psalms) This Holy Book was revealed to the Prophet Daud (David) (PBUH).

The *Injil* (Gospels) This was a Holy Book revealed to the Prophet Isa (Jesus) (PBUH).

The Qur'an (Koran) This is the Holy Book (final message) to humankind which was revealed to the Prophet Muhammad (PBUH).

The Qur'an and previous Scripture

As Muslims, our humble submission on the previous Books, which were revealed before the Qur'an, is a simple one. God would send a fresh message (revelation) whenever the faith of the people was in decline. The message would urge people to repent and renew their covenant (submission) to the will of Allah. We further acknowledge that God revealed these previous Books to His prophets for the guidance of humankind. The Qur'an, like other Divine Books before it, is not a new and strange revelation. Far from it! The Qur'an is just the final revelation, which confirms earlier Scriptures, clears up all uncertainties, and perfects the truth. The Qur'an testifies that there have been earlier revelations before it. It says,

> He hath revealed unto thee (Muhammad) the Scripture with truth, confirming that which was (revealed) before it, even as He revealed the Torah and the Gospel aforetime, for a guidance to mankind. (Qur'an 3:3-4a)

The Qur'an really speaks very respectfully of all the prophets and messengers before Muhammad. Christians and Jews are referred to as *Ahl al-Kitab,* People of the Book. To these people the Qur'an admonishes,

> Say: O People of the Scripture! Ye have naught (of guidance) till ye observe the Torah and the Gospel and that which was revealed unto you from your Lord. (Qur'an 5:68)

The Qur'an further encourages Muslims to live amicably with the People of the Book and even marry their women. The Holy Qur'an teaches,

> The food of those who have received the Scripture is lawful for you, and your food is lawful for them. And so are the virtuous women of the believers and the virtuous women of those who received the Scripture before you. (Qur'an 5:5)

The previous Divine Scriptures (Books) having been revealed by Allah, naturally taught people righteousness, love, and the way of life that is most pleasing to Allah. However, some of their commands and teachings seem to have been confined to a particular tribe, community, or nation, and to a specific period.

Furthermore, Muslims are aware that human imperfections seem to be included in the Bible. For example, the personalities of the biblical Prophets form part of the content of biblical Scriptures. Moreover, the biblical Scriptures include both history and the Word of God. The Bible seems to be a mixture of history and revelation. Therefore, it is extremely difficult to separate the true revelation in the Bible from the history and the human personality which the Bible also contains.

Therefore, the Qur'an, as the final revelation, is the perfection and culmination of all the truth contained in the earlier Scriptures (revelations). Though sent in Arabic, it is the Book for all times and for all humankind. The purpose of the Qur'an is to guard the previous revelations by restoring the eternal truth of Allah. The Qur'an is the torchlight by which humanity can be rightly guided onto the straight path.

The nature of the Holy Qur'an

The Qur'an is a unique Book of Divine guidance. The Qur'an is the very Word of Allah. It was revealed to the Prophet Muhammad (PBUH), through the archangel *Jibril* (Gabriel) from an archetype preserved in the seventh heaven. "Nay, but it is a glorious Qur'an on a guarded tablet" (Qur'an 85:21-22). The Prophet Muhammad (PBUH) was the instrument chosen by Allah for the revelation of His Word. Every letter, word, content form, and meaning of the

Qur'an is Divinely revealed. What is especially surprising is that the Qur'an was revealed to Muhammad who was unlettered.

The revelations began in this way: The Prophet Muhammad (PBUH) used to retire to a cave in Mount Hira a few miles outside Mecca (Makkah) for spiritual meditation. One night while at the Mount, he was suddenly awakened by the angel Jibril. The angel commanded him to recite (*Iqra*)! The Prophet, who was overtaken by fear, told the angel that he did not know how to read. The angel repeated the command and received a similar answer. Finally the angel pressed the trembling Muhammad (PBUH) and taught him to read the following:

> Read: In the name of thy Lord who createth,
> Createth man from a clot.
> Read: And thy Lord is the Most Bounteous,
> Who teacheth by the pen,
> Teacheth man that which he knew not.
> (Qur'an 96:1-5)

With the above words, the revelation of the Holy Qur'an had begun. The Divine Messenger from God gave the Prophet the power to retain and receive Allah's Book. That was about the year A.D. 610; the Prophet was about forty years old. The Qur'an was revealed portion by portion for a period of twenty-three years, which ended shortly before the Prophet's death in A.D. 632. The last verse to be sent by Allah said, "This day have I perfected your religion for you and completed My favor unto you, and have chosen for you as religion AL-ISLAM" (Qur'an 5:3). Between the first and last verses mentioned, the greatest Book in history was revealed to humankind.

The Qur'an is the most widely read book ever written. Muslims use it in worship, and it is the textbook from which all Muslims learn to read Arabic. It is the central reality in Islamic life. The Qur'an (a name derived from the word *recite*) is different from any other book. It is divided into 114 chapters (*surahs*), eighty-six of which were revealed to the Prophet while he was at Makkah, and twenty-eight at Madinah. The chapters are divided into *ayat* (verses), all of varying length. The three shortest surahs (103, 108,

110) have three verses each, while the longest surah, *al-Baqqara* (2), is divided into 286 verses. Every detail about the Qur'an has been carefully studied and recorded. For instance, it is known that the Qur'an contains 6,239 verses, 77,934 words, and 323,621 letters. It also has been discovered recently that the Qur'an is a mathematical miracle, all of it being based on multiples of the figure 19[1] ("over it are nineteen" Qur'an 74:30).

A stranger to the Qur'an would be struck by what appears a kind of incoherence from the human point of view. Unlike all other books, the Qur'an does not contain information, ideas, or arguments about specific themes arranged in a literary or serial order. Subjects are not discussed under specific topics. They are scattered all over the book. Yet to those who first received the revelation, there was no incoherence because it was relevant to their particular situation.

There is no subject which the Qur'an does not discuss. Theology, jurisprudence, science, and history are some of the major subjects the Qur'an deals with. That is why for many centuries the Qur'an has been the scientific manual and the textbook for acquiring liberal education in the Muslim world. Although the Qur'an does not describe all aspects of knowledge in complete detail, it is nevertheless the source and foundation of all true wisdom and knowledge. It is Allah's Word.

Although the Qur'an is not arranged in a chronological order, the arrangement was determined by Allah's will. This further emphasizes the Qur'an's uniqueness. Strangers to the Qur'an would benefit more if they realized that the Qur'an, being a Divine Book, is not to be compared with any form of human writing. It is a unique book whose literary style is quite different from all other known forms of literature. The subject it deals with is humankind. The central theme is the exposition of reality. The aim of the revelations is to invite humans to the straight path of true guidance, which they have lost through time, negligence, and other forms of evil. Anyone who studies the Qur'an, with the above three aspects (subject, central theme, and aim) in mind, discovers that there is no incoherence or any other shortcoming in the literary style of these Divine Scriptures.

Furthermore, the Qur'an is the most excellent Arabic poetry

and prose ever written or recited. When the unbelievers asked the Prophet Muhammad (PBUH) for proof that the Qur'an is the Word of Allah, he challenged them to produce only one verse or a line of Arabic of equal quality. None could meet his challenge. The Qur'an says,

> And if ye are in doubt concerning that which We reveal unto Our slave (Muhammad), then produce a surah of the like thereof, and call your witnesses beside Allah if ye are truthful. (Qur'an 2:23)

The unexcelled excellence of Qur'anic Arabic is one of the proofs of its Divine origin (Qur'an 12 :2).

Compilation of the Qur'an

Whenever the Prophet received a revelation, he memorized it before the angel Jibril. After ascertaining its proper recitation, Jibril told him in which order to place it. Then the Prophet instructed his scribes (for he did not know how to read or write) to record it under his supervision. Every recording was recited back for his verification. So the Prophet himself directed the proper recording and arrangement of the Qur'an as commanded by Allah. Soon the Qur'an was memorized by the companions of the Prophet for purposes of worship and interest. The Arabs, who had a warm taste for literature, found in the Qur'an a wonderful masterpiece of literature. By the time of the death of the Prophet, the Qur'an had already been preserved in people's memories and on various recording materials such as clay tablets, bones, the bark of trees, pieces of pottery, and stone.

In A.D. 632, after the death of the Prophet Muhammad (PBUH), Abu Bakr became the first Caliph (successor to the Prophet). Umar persuaded Abu Bakr to compile the Qur'an into one volume because many memorizers of the Qur'an (*Hafiz*) were disappearing from the scene through battles and natural death. Abu Bakr instructed Zaid Ibn Thabit, Muhammad's chief scribe of revelations, to collect and compile the entire Qur'an in the same order as authorized by the Prophet. This he did under close supervision and the help of the companions of the Prophet, who had memorized the entire Qur'an. The final version was checked and approved by all Muslims, who had heard the Qur'an from the Prophet. The Qur'an was still fresh in their memories as it was recorded in book form only two years after the death of the Prophet Muhammad (PBUH).

During the rule of the third Caliph, 'Uthman, it was reported that the Qur'an was being pronounced with different accents, especially by the non-Arab converts to Islam. 'Uthman's action was instantaneous. He recalled all copies of the Qur'an in circulation, and appointed a committee of four former scribes, including Zaid Ibn Thabit, to study the Qur'an further. The committee authorized one standard copy, which followed the dialect of the Quraish, which the Prophet himself had used. The Qur'an used today is the very same one as received by the Prophet, and authorized by Caliph 'Uthman and the companions (*sahaba*) of the Prophet in A.D. 651. No word, order, or punctuation mark has been changed, omitted, or added. Even God testifies to the purity of the Qur'an when He says, "Lo! We, even We, reveal the Reminder, and lo! We verily are its Guardian" (Qur'an 15:9).

Hadith

Islam can be understood through two main sources: (1) The Holy Qur'an and (2) the collections of the recorded words, actions, and sanctions of the Prophet Muhammad (PBUH). These acts (*sunnah*) and sayings (*hadith*) of the Prophet are collectively known as the *Hadith*.

The sunnah (acts), and hadith (sayings) show the way of life of the Prophet Muhammad (PBUH). Sunnah means the practices and way of life of the Prophet, and hadith means the reports of what the Prophet taught or said. The collection of writings known as the Hadith include both sunnah and hadith. A report or verbal tradition transmitted by word of mouth about what the Prophet said, did, or how he reacted to others (sunnah or hadith) is called a hadith and the written collection are called the Hadith. When a companion of the Prophet saw him do something, e.g. praying, he reported it to his friends, who in turn reported it to others, and thus the report continued. Many companions tried to write down hadith for their own custody, but they were stopped by the Prophet lest they confuse them with the Qur'an.

Later the science of hadith was developed, whereby collections of hadith were compiled. In this case each report had to be prefaced by a chain of narrators (*isnad*), who were known to be mature, pious, intelligent, and reliable. The text (*matn*) which the narrators transmitted also had to be intelligible and credible. The process of collecting the hadith was practically completed during the second century of the Muslim era. As a result of the exercise, we now have well-documented books with all the necessary information about the Prophet Muhammad (PBUH).

The Hadith is not a Holy Book (revelation) as the Qur'an and the previous Scriptures. However, to the Muslims the importance of Hadith ranks only second to the Holy Qur'an. The Hadith is complementary to the Qur'an. It helps to explain and clarify the Holy Qur'an and to present the Qur'an in a more practical form. The Qur'an witnesses thus: "Whoso obeyeth the messenger obeyeth Allah" (Qur'an 4:80; also 33:21, 7:157, 14:44). As Muslims, our knowledge of Islam would be incomplete and shaky if we did not study and follow the Hadith. Similarly an outsider cannot understand Islam if he ignores the Hadith.

Summary

Muslims believe that God revealed His Word to some of His prophets and messengers for the guidance of humankind. All revelation, which has given guidance to humans, needs to be renewed whenever the faith of a people is in decline. These revelations have come to us in the form of Holy Books. All the previous Books revealed by God must be accepted as true. However, the Qur'an is the final revelation, which confirms earlier Scriptures and perfects the truth. The Hadith, though not a Holy Scripture, is complementary to the Holy Qur'an.

A CHRISTIAN RESPONSE

Christians and Muslims are people of Scripture. Both have an exceedingly high regard for the Word of God. Muslims respect the Bible in its original form with special mention of the Taurat (Torah) of the Prophet Moses, the Zabur (Psalms) of the Prophet David, and the Injil (Gospel) of Jesus the Messiah All three of these Scriptures are contained in the Bible. The value which Muslims place on these

Scriptures is revealed in the Qur'anic warning to Christians and Jews that they should not hide their Scriptures but make their Scriptures available to humankind (Qur'an 3:71). Christians are thankful that Muslims have a respect for the Bible.

Nevertheless, Muslims and Christians should reflect carefully together on the nature and meaning of revelation. Does not all divine revelation have an incarnational quality? Is not God's revealed Word to humankind always expressed through human personality, in human language and thought forms? Furthermore, we need to ask ourselves what criteria determine which books are truly the revealed word of God.

Christians believe that the central fact of divine revelation is God's self-disclosure. God reveals himself preeminently through his acts in human history. Divine Scriptures are, therefore, a revelation of God's self-disclosure, and the divinely inspired record of man's response to God's self-disclosure. Christians do not perceive of revelation as divine books sent down from heaven, but rather as the personal Word of God engaged in lively, active encounter with people. That is the nature of biblical revelation .

Christians believe it is exceedingly important to receive and believe the message of the entire Bible. It is necessary to read the entire Bible so we can receive God's message to humankind. Christians do not believe some books are revealed for a particular people for a particular time. Jesus the Messiah used the holy writings of many prophets in his preaching and urged his followers to "search the Scriptures." All inspired Scripture belongs together. Each portion of the Bible is needed to understand God's full revelation to humankind. Furthermore, no portion of divine Scripture contains all the truth we need to know.

A MUSLIM CLARIFICATION

Muslims must and do believe in all the original Books of God which have been revealed to humankind. Muslims also believe that all the universal aspects of previous revelations have been summarized in the Qur'an. In the Qur'an all the universal aspects of Divine guidance have been preserved exactly as revealed to the Prophet Muhammad (PBUH).

Note

1. Ahmad Deedat, *Al-Qur'an: the Ultimate Miracle* (Durban: 4001, Islamic Propagation Centre, Madressa Arcade, 1979), pp. 1-75.

In the Name of Allah, the Compassionate, the Merciful.

6
The Prophets of Allah

THE MUSLIM UNDERSTANDING

Muslims usually make a distinction between a "Prophet" and a "messenger" of Allah. The messenger (*rasul*) is sent with Divine Scripture to guide and reform humankind; he is given a Divine Book. The Prophet (*al nabbi*) carries information or proclaims Allah's news. The Prophets are not given Books like the messengers. Although all messengers are Prophets, not all Prophets are messengers. Both messengers and Prophets are people chosen by God to deliver His message, which is given by means of Divine revelation (*Wahy*). This Divine message is for the guidance of a group of people, a nation, or the whole of humankind.

The nature of Prophets

Allah has bestowed the important office of prophethood on some of His servants according to His wish. They were chosen to guide their communities and humankind onto the straight path of Allah. They all brought essentially the same message—Islam. God gave them greater knowledge about His will, His religion, the human heart, and good and evil. They guided humankind, taught them to live happily in this world and to be prepared for life after death.

All Prophets were human beings. They could eat, drink, walk, sleep, speak, breathe, suffer, and face problems like all of us do. They were intelligent, trustworthy, knowledgeable, and most obedient to God. They were the best examples of moral trust, as the Qur'an says: "It is not for any Prophet to deceive (mankind). . ." (Qur'an 3:161). Allah protected them from serious sins and bad diseases.

It is because the Prophets were human that their witness was received with mixed feelings and even total rejection among their own communities. The Qur'an says, "And naught prevented mankind from believing when the guidance came unto them save that they said: Hath Allah sent a mortal as (His) messenger?" (Qur'an 17:94).

As Muslims we must not make the mistake of condemning any of Allah's Prophets as impostors or uplifting any into a superhuman being. The Prophet Muhammad (PBUH), like other Prophets before him, emphasized his human nature. The Qur'an testifies, "Muhammad is but a messenger, messengers (the like of whom) have passed away before him" (Qur'an 3:144). In another verse Allah says, "Say: I am only a mortal like you My Lord inspireth in me that your God is only One God" (Qur'an 18:111). Muslims must have faith in all Allah's Prophets. Denying the prophethood of any one of them constitutes disbelief.

As already observed, God sent a large number of Prophets at various stages of history for the proper guidance of humankind. These Prophets were raised from among almost every people as is witnessed by the Qur'an: "And verily We have raised in every nation a messenger (proclaiming): Serve Allah and shun false gods" (Qur'an 16:36). The Qur'an further states,

> Say (Muslims): We believe in Allah and that which is revealed unto us and that which was revealed unto Abraham, and Ishmael, and Isaac, and Jacob, and the tribes, and that which Moses and Jesus received, and that which the Prophets received from their Lord. We make no distinction between any of them, and unto Him we have surrendered. (Qur'an 2:136)

The exact number of Allah's Prophets is not clear, but Muslim tradition has put it at 124,000. The Qur'an mentions only twenty-five Prophets, but Muslims must believe even in those not mentioned. Allah says, "And messengers We have mentioned unto thee before and messengers We have not mentioned unto thee . . ." (Qur'an 4:164).

The following are the names of those Prophets mentioned in the Holy Qur'an: Adam, Saleh, Lut (Lot), Hud, Y'acub (Jacob), Ibrahim (Abraham), Yunus (Jonah), Musa (Moses), Daud (David),

Al-Ya'sa (Elisha), Zakara (Zachariah), Dhul-Kifl (Ezekiel), Isa (Jesus), Nuhu (Noah), Shu'aib, Ismai'il (Ishmael), Yusuf (Joseph), Ishaq (Isaac), Harun (Aaron), Sulaiman (Solomon), Yahya (John the Baptist), Ayyub (Job), Ilyas (Elijah), Idrees, Muhammad, (Peace be upon all of them).

Muhammad (PBUH) is the last Prophet and messenger of Allah. His mission was for the whole world and for all times.

The role of Prophets in history

Adam, the first man on earth, was also the first Prophet of Allah. God revealed the religion of Islam to Adam, which is submission to the one true God, the Creator, Sustainer of the world, Lord of the universe, and Master of the day of judgment. God made it clear to Adam that humans should worship and obey only Allah, the most Exalted. This is the covenant of submission which God gave to Adam: God the Master, and humankind the servant (*abd*).

Some of Adam's offspring who were righteous followed Allah's teaching, but others drifted into evil activities. They compromised the true guidance by associating Allah with other gods and objects. To provide humankind with firm and constructive guidance, God raised Prophets among every people. The fundamental message proclaimed by all Prophets was the same. They taught or reminded people of the unity of God; the reward of leading a good, pious, and peaceful life; the day of judgment; and the terrible punishment for unbelievers. All Prophets brought this same message (Islam) from Allah. They set good examples with their own lives. They had to demonstrate by practice the faith which they followed.

The Prophets tried to establish a divinely sanctioned moral code, social justice, and co-operation among their fellow humans— i.e., a complete way of life. In the process of establishing God's command on earth, some Prophets were successful and others were not. Many people were intolerant of God's Prophets. They mistreated the Prophets by punishing them, torturing them, and refusing to listen to or accept their teachings. Despite opposition, the Prophets never gave up or compromised Allah's truth; their mission was not a complete failure.

Some of the Prophets are especially noteworthy. For instance, the Prophet Ibrahim's (Abraham) major achievement was the proc-lamation of the oneness of Allah. This is a belief that has been main-tained for several thousand years. Islam acknowledges the Prophet Musa (Moses) as the one to whom Allah spoke: "And Allah spake directly unto Moses" (Qur'an 4:164). Moses is given the title "Kalim-ullah," which means the one to whom God spoke. Never-theless, important as Moses' message was, his people believed the guidance was intended only for them. They have also added too many ritualistic details to the original law of Moses. Like all Proph-ets before him, Isa (Jesus) son of Mary preached the Oneness of Allah. The Christians received the universal message of God, but have compromised it by stressing the "trinity" instead of the "uni-ty" of Allah.

At last God has sent His final guidance to all humankind through the Prophet Muhammad (PBUH). The truth that all the previous Prophets had proclaimed to humanity was perfected by the Prophet Muhammad (PBUH). The Qur'an, which is Allah's fi-nal guidance to humankind, was revealed to the Prophet Muham-mad (PBUH), the Seal of all Prophets, six hundred years after the Prophet Isa (PBUH). Muhammad (PBUH) is the one Prophet who fulfilled Allah's mission during his lifetime. The last message from Allah to Muhammad said, "This day have I perfected your religion for you and completed My favor unto you, and have chosen for you as religion AL-ISLAM" (Qur'an 5:3). So Muhammad (PBUH) was Allah's last messenger through whom the original religion of hu-mans—Islam—was completed and perfected and a community of Muslims established.

Summary
Muslims believe in and respect all the Prophets of God who preceded Muhammad (PBUH). They all brought a uniform mes-sage—Islam—from Allah. Muhammad is the last and the seal of Prophethood. Through him, Islam was completed and perfected. As he brought the last and latest guidance for all humankind, it is he alone to whom Muslims turn for guidance.

A CHRISTIAN RESPONSE
Both Muslims and Christians believe in Prophets. The writings and

teachings of at least thirty Prophets and apostles are included in the Bible. The names of many of the biblical Prophets are mentioned in the Qur'an. Moses is one of the greatest Prophets of the Bible.

It would be good for Christians and Muslims to reflect together on the meanings of God's encounter with Moses at the burning bush, an event both the Bible and the Qur'an describe. In this event we recognize that God talked with Moses. Out of this encounter the biblical record reveals a new name for God: I AM, which is *Yahweh* in the Hebrew language. Beginning with the Prophet Moses, God progressively revealed himself as *Yahweh*—the God of covenant fellowship, the one who encounters humans personally. To get the full picture of God's self-revelation as Yahweh in the biblical Prophetic witness, it is necessary to open our lives to the total Prophetic witness.

The message of the Prophets is like a great and beautiful building. The early Prophets such as Abraham and Moses laid a foundation for the building. Later Prophets such as David and Isaiah formed the walls of the building. The Prophet Jesus, the Messiah, is like the roof on the building. All the biblical Prophets taken together form a beautiful building. Christians earnestly and humbly give witness that all people should read and accept the message of all the true Prophets of God. Every part of the building is important. All are needed to understand God's full revelation to humankind.

A MUSLIM CLARIFICATION

From a Muslim perspective, it is advisable not to carry the event of the Prophet Moses (PBUH) and the burning bush too far. Although God spoke to the Prophet Moses (PBUH) from the burning bush, some Muslim scholars believe that it was the Angel Jibril who was present in the bush. At the same time, Muslims would affirm that the name Allah is the most profound revealed name for the Almighty. Muslims would witness that we cannot do better than to refer to God by that name of surpassing beauty which He Himself has revealed to the last Prophet, Muhammad (PBUH).

In the Name of Allah, the Compassionate, the Merciful.

7
The Seal of Prophets

THE MUSLIM WITNESS CONCERNING THE PROPHET MUHAMMAD (PBUH)

Muhammad[1] was born in the commercial city of Makkah (Mecca), Arabia, on 12 Rabi Awwal (or Monday, 20 August) A.D. 570. His mother was Amina bint Wahab, who hailed from Madinah (Medina). His father, Abdallah, was one of the many sons of Abdul-Muttalib, head of the noble family of Banu Hashim, a branch of the Quraish tribe. Abdul-Muttalib was also the chief guardian of the sanctuary of the Ka'bah, which is the House of God in Makkah, wherein the sacred black stone is located.

As a child, Muhammad (PBUH) was unfortunate. His father had died a few months before his birth. At age six, he lost his mother. Then his grandfather, Abdul-Muttalib, took care of him, but he too died only two years later. So at age eight, Muhammad (PBUH) was orphaned. However, interested relatives were not lacking. He was soon taken over by his uncle, Abu Talib, son of Abdul-Muttalib. The uncle loved his nephew. He gave him good care.

Muhammad (PBUH) spent the early years of his youth with his uncle. He helped his uncle with his work enthusiastically. Muhammad (PBUH) loved and appreciated work. He could do work of any kind without any ill feelings. He mended his clothes and shoes. He tended sheep, goats, and camels, and accompanied his uncle on caravans. He traveled to Syria twice, the first trip being made when he was only twelve. Muhammad (PBUH) had no formal schooling. He did not know how to read and write. Nevertheless, as a youth he was respected and admired by the natives of Makkah for his uprightness, honesty, and good behavior. Hence he was given the title al-Amin (the trustworthy).

The society Muhammad (PBUH) was born into

The society in which Muhammad (PBUH) lived before his mission is called *jahiliyya*—the period of ignorance and darkness. The Arabs were polytheists with a poor notion of a high god—Allah. They worshiped a pantheon of gods, but the most important ones acknowledged by the Makkahn Quraish were al-Uzza, al-Manat, and al-Lat, who were referred to as daughters of Allah. The Ka'bah (the House of Allah in Makkah) had been polluted with all sorts of evil. It was now home of 360 idol gods symbolizing all the Arab gods, and a different one was worshiped each day of the year.

Wine drinking, gambling, raiding, and blood feuds were the order of the day. The women performed naked dances and composed poems describing every member of the body. There was no respect for women. Baby daughters were suspected of bringing bad luck, and some fathers buried them alive immediately after birth. Property was what mattered, for one's worth was measured by how much one had. This was the society Muhammad (PBUH) grew up in.

Muhammad (PBUH) hated this corrupt society, even as a child. As a man of high moral and spiritual caliber, Muhammad (PBUH) was perturbed by the evil ways and misery of his people. He started frequenting a cave in Mount Hira, a few miles outside Makkah, for meditation. All the same he continued in employment to earn a living.

Muhammad's (PBUH) marriage

As Abu Talib was a man of scanty means, he looked for a job for his nephew, Muhammad (PBUH). The wealthy merchant contacted was Lady Khadija bint Khuwaylid. She readily agreed to take on the trustworthy Muhammad (PBUH) as leader of her caravans. Khadija was twice widowed with two sons and a daughter. She was extremely wealthy. She found in her new employee an honest, kind, responsible, upright, and virtuous man. Muhammad (PBUH) had all the best qualities one could look for.

Attracted by Muhammad's (PBUH) rare qualities, Khadija offered to marry him. He agreed, and a wedding took place. He was twenty-five years old and Khadija was forty. The couple enjoyed twenty-five years of happy marriage until Khadija's death. Allah gave them seven children, but the three sons died in infancy and only the four daughters survived. In the end Muhammad (PBUH) was survived by only one daughter, Fatima, and she lived only six months longer than the Prophet.

After Muhammad's (PBUH) marriage to Khadija, he had more leisure, which enabled him to devote time to his spiritual quest The Qur'an testifies: "Did He not find thee an orphan and protect (thee)? Did He not find thee wandering and direct (thee)? Did He not find thee destitute and enrich (thee)?" (Qur'an 93:6-8).

Muhammad's (PBUH) Prophethood (Risalat)

As earlier stated, Muhammad (PBUH) used to visit the cave (*ghar*) of Hira frequently for spiritual meditation. It was during one night in the month of Ramadhan that he heard a mighty voice commanding him to recite in the name of Allah Who creates (Qur'an 96:1-5). This night of revelation is remembered in Muslim history as the Night of Power (*Lailatu-l-Qadr*). This was about the year A.D. 610, and the Prophet Muhammad (PBUH) was forty years old. The first revelation had descended on Muhammad (PBUH) through the angel Jibril (Gabriel). In this way Muhammad (PBUH) was appointed by Allah to be His last Prophet (Qur'an 33:40)

Muhammad (PBUH), overcome with fear, hurried home and related to his beloved Khadija all that had happened. She comforted him, assuring him that what he had received was true revelation from Allah. She was the first person in Makkah to accept Islam.

The first revelation was followed shortly by a second one, which came to Muhammad (PBUH) when he was shivering and had been covered by a mantle at home. The command was, "O thou enveloped in thy cloak, Arise and warn! Thy Lord magnify" (Qur'an 74:1-3). Muhammad (PBUH), through Allah's Word, had been chosen to spread His message.

Muhammad (PBUH) began his mission quietly. He preached the Oneness of God. He stressed that Allah is all-powerful. He is the Creator of the universe and the Master of the day of judgment. On the day of judgment, the faithful and righteous will be rewarded with paradise, while the unbelievers and the idolaters will end up in hell—an abode of great torture and suffering.

In all Muhammad's (PBUH) teaching, he made it clear that he

was not superhuman or an incarnation of God, but only a human being and a messenger of Allah. The Qur'an testifies to Muhammad's (PBUH) human nature. "Say: For myself I have no power to benefit, nor power to hurt, save that which Allah willeth. . . . I am but a warner, and a bearer of good tidings unto folk who believe" (Qur'an 7:188) .

In the first three years, Muhammad (PBUH) had only converted a few Makkans. Important names among them were Khadija, his wife; Ali, his young cousin; Abu Bakr, 'Uthman, and Talha—all his friends. Soon Muhammad (PBUH) was commanded by Allah to preach in public. He consequently went to Mount Safa, opposite the *Ka'bah* in Makkah, where he firmly declared the Oneness of Allah. He poured scorn on the idols the Makkans worshiped and subsequently invited them to submit only to the One true God— Allah. He warned all those who would not submit to God's judgment, "Nay, but they deny (the coming of) the Hour, and for those who deny (the coming of) the Hour We have prepared a flame" (Qur'an 25:11).

Opposition and persecution

Muhammad's (PBUH) preaching annoyed many citizens of Makkah. They realized that his preaching would curb their power and economic interests as guardians of the al-Ka'bah. They threatened him, but he would not waver. They tried to bribe him with wealth, women, and even kingship to give up his preaching, but they failed miserably to entice him. Open persecution was the last alternative, and they soon resorted to that. Some of the converts to Islam, like Bilal or Khabbab, were scorched on the hot desert sands with heavy burning stones on their chests. Many Muslims were beaten to death. Even the Prophet did not escape persecution. Thorns were spread along his path and rubbish thrown over his back. In Taif, a town to the north of Makkah, the Prophet Muhammad (PBUH) was stoned until he bled.

Regardless of persecutions, more people embraced Islam. As a result of the continuing severe persecution, the Prophet advised eleven families to migrate to the Christian kingdom of Abyssinia, then under the rule of King Negus. They were well received and protected. The first group of exiles was joined later by eighty-three others, who included 'Uthman bin 'Affan, who later became the third Caliph of Islam. Efforts by the Quraish unbelievers of Makkah to have the Muslims repatriated failed completely. King Negus would not hand over, to the pagan Quraish, the Muslims, who believed in one God, and all His Prophets, including Jesus.

Despite the loss of his devout followers, Muhammad (PBUH) continued to preach and get converts. Revelation also continued to pour on him. About this time, two great figures of Islam embraced the faith. They were 'Umar, who later became the second Caliph of Islam, and Hamza, the Prophet's uncle. 'Umar, who was respected and feared by all the Quraish, started conducting his prayers to Allah in the Ka'bah. This stunned and vexed the Quraish, who vowed to increase their persecution of Muslims and their leader.

The Quraish demanded that the Banu Hashim (Muhammad's [PBUH] family) hand him over or face the consequences. The Banu Hashim led by Muhammad's (PBUH) uncle, Abu Talib, refused. Consequently they were boycotted at the valley of Shu'ab-Abu Talib for three years. It was shortly after the trying boycott that Abu Talib died. Though Abu Talib never embraced Islam, he stood firm to the very end in defense of his nephew. As if that were not enough of a blow, at about that time the Prophet also lost his beloved wife, Khadija. The Prophet described this experience as the year of "sorrow."

The Prophet and the Mir'aj

About this same time, a number of people from Madinah who had learned about Islam came to the Prophet in Makkah and embraced Islam. They invited him to come and stay with them in Madinah (then called Yathreb) under their oath of protection. The invitation was welcomed, but the Prophet did not accept it immediately.

In the meantime the Holy Prophet was taken on a night journey (*isra*) to heaven. He was transported from Makkah to Jerusalem on an animal called al-Buraq, then ascended (Mir'aj) to the seventh heaven.[2] Mir'aj was a physical as well as a spiritual journey. The Prophet, who had been greatly honored by Allah, was shown all that was in heaven and the universe. He saw the light and glory of God. This was the greatest gift from God to man.

It was during the Mir'aj that Allah commanded the five daily prayers for Muslims. The Prophet was given the honor of meeting all the earlier Prophets and leading them in prayer. This experience gave the Prophet much hope and strength in his year of sorrow in Makkah.

The Migration of the Prophet Muhammad (PBUH)

Realizing through experience the Divine guidance that the Quraish were determined to exterminate the Muslims, Muhammad (PBUH) allowed two hundred of his followers to take refuge in Yathreb (Madinah), where they had been already invited. He himself followed later, evading the hot pursuit of the Quraish. He was accompanied by his life companion, Abu Bakr. He arrived in Yathreb on 24 September, A.D. 622. This migration from Makkah to Yathreb is known as the *Hijrah*.

The arrival of the Prophet in Yathreb brought great jubilation to the townsmen. In fact, the name of the city was changed from Yathreb to Madinatu 'an-nabi—the City of the Prophet. The short form is Madinah. Sixteen years later, Caliph 'Umar designated the year of Hijrah as the official starting point of the Muslim era.

The Hijrah is a very significant event. The Qur'an teaches, And when those who disbelieve plot against thee (O Muhammad) to wound thee fatally, or to kill thee or to drive thee forth; they plot, but Allah (also) plotteth; and Allah is the best of plotters. (Qur'an 8 :30)
Thus the Hijrah saw the beginning of a new era.

The Muslims who migrated from Makkah were called the Muhajirun (emigrants or followers), and those who welcomed them in Madinah were called the *Ansar* (helpers). The Muhajirun and the Ansar were now united under the faith of Islam and the leadership of the Prophet. This was how the first Muslim community (*Umma*) was formed. (This will be discussed in another chapter.) In Madinah the Prophet was not only the leader of the Muslim community but also of non-Muslims. He was now a Prophet and statesman, and he continued to receive more revelations, which dealt especially with legislative and administrative matters. For instance, Ramadhan was prescribed as the month of fasting, and the

Qibla (direction of prayer) was changed from Jerusalem to Makkah.

The new community faced many problems caused by the enemies of Islam. There were enemies who lived among the Muslims
and even outside Madinah. Many people treacherously colluded
with the Quraish to destroy the Muslims. Given the precarious situation, the Muslim community stood on guard and took strong measures to deal with their enemies.

The Quraish of Makkah, still burning with the desire to exterminate the Muslims, sent their army of one thousand men to meet
the Muslims. This was in A.D. 624 (2 A.H.). The Muslims could
only field three hundred soldiers. The two armies met at Badr, and
by Allah's will the Muslims, under the inspiring leadership of the
Prophet, quickly routed the Makkans. This was a moral and spiritual victory for the Muslims.

A year later, the Quraish again attacked the Muslims in the fa-
mous battle of Uhud. This time the unbelievers were victorious in
battle but suffered so many casualties they could not follow up
their victory. In the end the Muslims turned them back. Yet again in
A.D. 627, the Quraish attacked Madinah and besieged it. Allah was
with the Muslims, for later the Quraish withdrew.

In A.D. 628 the Prophet led fourteen hundred Muslims to his
mother city (Makkah) for worship. He made a treaty of Hudaibiyya
with the Makkan Quraish. By this treaty, Makkans and Muslims
were to be treated on equal terms. Furthermore, the Makkans
agreed to vacate the city of Makkah for three days while the Muslims entered for worship. There were many other intricate articles
of the treaty. The treaty was very lenient to the Quraish unbelievers.

However, the Quraish broke their part of the treaty, and the
Prophet moved on to Makkah with the Muslim forces. He quickly
took over without resistance in January A.D. 630 (8 A.H.). On en-
tering the city, he uttered this Qur'anic verse: "Truth hath come
and falsehood hath vanished away" (Qur'an 17:81). He then
smashed all the 360 idols that had surrounded the Ka'bah. To his
enemies, who were so worried about their fate, he said, "No blame
is on you this day. Go to your homes, for you are all free." [3] This
was a good lesson for Muslims on how to treat their defeated enemies.

On 23 February, A.D. 632 (10 A.H.) the Prophet, accompanied by fourteen thousand Muslims, made his farewell pilgrimage to Makkah. In his last sermon at Arafat, he spoke concerning fifteen social aspects which affect everyone's human relationships. He emphasized the Oneness and unity of God, the importance of Allah's message, the day of judgment, the sanctity of life, respect for Prophets, respect for women, respect for slaves, and the importance of the Muslim brotherhood. He told the Umma that he had bequeathed to them two things: the Book of God and the *Sunnah* (practice) of His messenger. It was about this time when he received the last revelation, which we have already mentioned (Qur'an 5:3).

It was exactly three months after the farewell pilgrimage that the Prophet was taken ill. At exactly noon, on Monday, 8 June, A.D, 632 (twelfth Rabil Awwal 11 A.H.), while in prayer, the last Prophet and messenger of Allah died. His death was a trying moment for all Muslims.

Abu Bakr's comment on the death of the Prophet was well presented and most effective. To the grief-stricken Muslim community, he said, "If you worshiped Muhammad, he is indeed dead; but if you worship God, He is alive and can never die."[4]

Muhammad (PBUH) —the Seal of Prophets

As already mentioned, the Qur'an and Muhammad (PBUH) himself made it clear that he, Muhammad (PBUH), is a human being. He is neither God nor His son but just the last Prophet of God who has been sent to show guidance to all humankind. The Qur'an says,

> Say (O Muhammad): O mankind! I am the messenger of Allah to you all—(the messenger of) Him unto whom belongeth the Sovereignty of the heavens and the earth.
> . . . So believe in Allah and His messenger, the Prophet who can neither read nor write, . . . and follow him that haply ye may be led aright. (Qur'an 7:158)

We also learn from the Qur'an that the Prophet Muhammad (PBUH) has been sent as a mercy to all God's creatures, human and non-human: "We sent thee not save as a mercy for the peoples" (Qur'an 21:107).

Muhammad's (PBUH) message was a logical completion and perfection of all the previous revelations. God, through the Qur'an and the Prophet, has emphasized the finality of Muhammad's (PBUH) Prophethood. The Qur'an says, "Muhammad is not the father of any man among you, but he is the messenger of Allah and the Seal of the Prophets; and Allah is Aware of all things" (Qur'an 33:40). Allah has taught us that Muhammad (PBUH) has closed (sealed) the long line of His apostles.

Who is able to oppose the Qur'anic teaching? As Muslims we believe in the Qur'an and whatever it says as the absolute truth. Now that Prophethood has come to a complete end, the later ages will need no Prophets, but pious men, revivers, reformers, and thinkers.

A CHRISTIAN RESPONSE

The Christian interpretation of the Prophet Muhammad should be determined by the whole biblical witness concerning Jesus the Messiah. Christians and Muslims agree that Jesus is the Messiah. What does it mean for Jesus to be the Messiah? The biblical witness is that the Messiah is the fulfillment of all the Scriptures and the Prophets. Christians believe that he is the Savior of humankind. The Messiah himself said, "I am the way, the truth, and the life" (John 14:6). Therefore Christians believe that the touchstone of all truth is Jesus the Messiah. That is the biblical witness.

Thus when a Christian looks at the Prophet Muhammad, he needs to evaluate Muhammad in light of the total biblical witness culminating in Jesus the Messiah. To the extent that the Prophet Muhammad accepts the total biblical witness and the central significance of Jesus the Messiah, and to the extent that the life and teachings of Muhammad give witness to the revelation of suffering, redemptive love which we perceive in Jesus the Messiah, Christians should appreciate and affirm the Prophet Muhammad.

A MUSLIM CLARIFICATION

Muslims do respect the Messiah, Jesus, profoundly. However, they do not believe that he is therefore superior to all other Prophets. In fact, the Qur'an affirms that Jesus foretold the coming of the Seal of the Prophets. The Qur'an says that Jesus came "bringing good tidings of a messenger who cometh after me, whose name is the Praised One" (i.e., either Ahmad or Muhammad) (Qur'an 61:6).

Notes

1. Muhammad when translated into English means "the Praised One."

2. Because Jerusalem served as the earthly station on this wonderful journey, it has remained the third holiest city in the Muslim world.

3. Ibn Sa'd, *Kitab al-Tabaqat*, Series II, Vol. 2 (Leiden, 1330 A.H.), pp. 54-55.

4. Hadith recorded by Ibn Ishaq-Ibn Hisham, Serat Rasul Allah (A. Guillaume's translation) p. 683.

In the Name of Allah, the Compassionate, the Merciful.

8
The Umma

THE MUSLIM COMMUNITY

The Muslim community is called the *Umma*. The Umma is different from any other community. It is not centered on tribe, nationality, race, or linguistic grouping. The Umma does not take its name from the founder or an event. The Umma is the community of Allah. He is the Absolute Truth to which the Muslim community owes its life and existence. The life and activities of the Umma are all under His legislative direction. Equally, the life of the individual member of the Umma, both private and public, is under God's legal command. It is Allah's Law which must be supreme in the Umma. What God has recommended as good for the community shall always remain good, and what He has forbidden shall always be denied. The Umma cannot authorize negation, deletion, or abrogation of Allah's supreme Law and scheme of values.

The Umma is divinely established by God, as the Qur'an witnesses: "And there may spring from you a nation who invite to goodness, and enjoin right conduct and forbid indecency. Such are they who are successful" (Qur'an 3:104). In another Qur'anic verse Allah praises the Umma in the following words: "Ye are the best community that hath been raised up for mankind. Ye enjoin right conduct and forbid indecency; and ye believe in Allah" (Qur'an 3:110).

This means that the Muslim community promotes virtue and abhors vice. The community stands for justice and righteousness. The Qu'ran teaches,

> O ye who believe! Be ye staunch in justice, witnesses for Allah, even though it be against yourselves or (your) parents or (your)

kindred, whether (the case be of) a rich man or a poor man, for Allah is nearer unto both (than ye are). (Qur'an 4:135)

Justice is a cherished virtue of the Umma. We further learn from the Hadith that one of the greatest *jihads* (striving in the path of Allah) is the word of justice said to an unjust leader. The Umma is also held together through the principle of unity and equality. The enforcement of the Muslim brotherhood is the greatest social ideal of Islam. The Qur'an states, "The believers are naught else than brothers" (Qur'an 49:10).

Muhammad (PBUH) and the Umma

In the seventh chapter, we saw how Muhammad (PBUH) migrated from Makkah in A.D. 622 and went to settle in Madinah. Here he was enthusiastically welcomed by the Madinah Muslims and the many exiles whom he had earlier sent from Makkah. The people of Madinah (especially the Aws and Khazraj who had earlier invited him) were happy that the Prophet had come at last to live with them. The emigrants from Makkah were given the title Muhajirun (exiles), while their hosts in Madinah were referred to as the Ansar (helpers). The Ansar and Muhajirun readily accepted the Prophet Muhammad (PBUH) as their head.

The first task, which the Prophet undertook in his new home, was to build a mosque at Quba for the worship of Allah, according to the Islamic principles. This was the first mosque to be built for the Umma. It was also the first mosque in history. This marked a turning point in the history of his mission and the Umma.

His second task in Madinah was to provide for the Muhajirun from Makkah, who had come with scanty possessions. The Ansar shared everything in their possession with the Muhajirun. Through this beautiful expression of brotherhood, the lives of the two parties were cohesively welded into one community.

Now that the Muslims were not in immediate danger from the Quraish of Makkah, the Prophet had ample time to organize his new community according to the Divine Law. He created a strong Umma in Madinah by Allah's will. During the first phase of the formative period of the Umma, the Prophet extended the authority of the Umma beyond the circles of the Muslim believers. This was logical because there were a number of people in Madinah under the Prophet who had not yet accepted Islam. The Exiles, the Helpers, and the Jews were the most important groups. To all these three groups, the Prophet granted their status, rights, and obligations.

The Prophet wrote a charter which regulated relationships among the different groups in Madinah. The Prophet's charter is one of the first written constitutions in the world. A thorough understanding of this charter might help one to appreciate why the enemies of the Muslims were effectively resisted by the Umma. The charter stated,

> In the name of Allah Most Merciful, Most Compassionate, this charter is given by Muhammad the Apostle of Allah, to all believers, whether Quraish or Madinan, and all individuals of whatever origin who have made common cause with them, who shall all constitute one nation (Umma).[1]

The conduct of individuals and the various groups in Madinah had to be based on this new charter and the subsequent relevant revelations. The charter stated that the Jews, who were part of the Islamic nation, would be protected from all insults and vexations. They would have equal rights with the Muslims and were free to practice their religion like the Muslims. Even the allies of the Jews would be given similar rights. The interior of Madinah was made sacred for all signatories to the charter. But the Jews and their allies had a duty, like Muslims, to defend the mother city, Madinah, against all enemies, Any who betrayed the Umma in any way had to be punished. All Muslims were to abhor every man found guilty of crime, injustice, disorder, or betrayal. The charter concluded by stating that all future disputes among the people of the charter would be referred under God, to the Prophet Muhammad (PBUH).[2]

In Madinah the mission of the Prophet was remarkably different from the Makkah period. Muhammad (PBUH) was no longer the persecuted Prophet; he was now the head of the Umma. He was the chief mediator and chief judge of the Umma. Muhammad (PBUH) never functioned by the conditional authority granted the tribe, which was typical of Arabian government in the *jahiliyya*. He ruled, rather, by absolute religious prerogative. The source of authority was not public opinion but Allah, who bestowed it on His Seal of Prophets. The Umma was a religious political unit—a theocracy. There was no distinction between what was purely religious and purely political, and there was no distinction between private and public conduct. Every institution of the Muslim society, political or social, had to conform to the *Shari'a*—the Law of God. For the same reason the Muslim army in Madinah was the army of Allah, and the Muslim treasury was the treasury of Allah.

While in Madinah the Prophet, who was also a statesman, continued to receive more revelations. The nature of revelation was rather different from that of Makkah. While the Makkan revelations centered mainly on faith, the revelations he received while in Madinah covered a broader range. They dealt with human conduct, including food and drink, marriage and family life, morals and manners, peace and war, trade and commerce, contracts, jihad (striving in the way of Allah) and crime and punishment. At the same time, the Prophet exemplified all he had preached by personal, practical, outward expression of faith and duty.

In Madinah the Prophet established some important institutions. Prayer (*salat*) was to be performed five times a day, preceded by *adhan* (call to prayer). *Saum* (fasting) was practiced in the sacred month of Ramadhan. Friday was substituted for the Jewish Sabbath. The *al-Ka'bah* in Makkah became the *Qibla* (direction of prayer). These practices gave cohesion to the Umma, which has never relied on an ordained hierarchy of priesthood. In Madinah the Holy Prophet created an Umma which transcended all ethnic and parochial loyalties.

Problems of the early Umma

Although the Muslims had succeeded in establishing a state (Umma), there were enemies from within and without. The first group of enemies was that of the "hypocrite Muslims" (*Munafiqun*). These had somehow entered the fold of Islam, but they still retained a concealed belief in idolatry They were tolerated, but when their leader, Abdallah Ibn Ubay, died, the group disappeared. Secondly, the Jews soon showed that they had accepted Muhammad's (PBUH) protection only from motives of temporary expediency.

They wished evil on the Muslims and through treachery colluded with the Quraish of Makkah, who were determined to destroy the nascent Umma. The Muslims, aware of the discontented elements in the Madinah Umma, kept a watch on their enemies, and at times they had to take effective measures in dealing with them.

In the second year of the *Hijrah*, the Makkahn Quraish fielded a strong force of one thousand soldiers to crush the Umma in Madinah. The Umma, which had the right to defend itself, hastily marched an ill-equipped force of only three hundred believers. The armies met at the Battle of Badr, eighty miles from Madinah. In the Battle of Badr, the purified army of Allah soon routed that of the infidels, although the infidel army was more than three times the size of the army of Allah. This amazing victory gave a lot of moral and spiritual support to the Umma. Justice, truth, and right had prevailed over evil.

Nevertheless, the humiliated infidels of Makkah were still determined to wipe out the Umma from Madinah. Twice, in A.D. 625 and 627, they marched against Madinah, and on both occasions failed to destroy the Muslim community. However, despite all these obstacles, the Umma succeeded in taking over the whole of the Arabian Peninsula after only a decade of hard struggle.

The spread of the Umma

By the time of the death of the Prophet Muhammad (PBUH) in A.D. 632, the Umma was well established in Arabia. The Prophet had been aware of the universal nature of his mission. The Umma was not to be restricted to the Arabs only. The whole world had to get the message of Islam. He therefore made arrangements to send his Muslim envoys to Syria and Egypt. He invited the leaders and their subjects to embrace Islam. The envoys were received with mixed feelings.

As Islam spread, the Umma, which was essentially based on Islamic law, was quickly transformed from an Arab Umma into a universal Muslim Umma. It is not surprising that the Umma extended very quickly, after the Prophet's death, far beyond the confines of the Arabian Peninsula. In the process, it brought together peoples of different cultures, races, and nations to form one great Umma. Today the Umma is still spreading. The universal message of reform (Islam) is now embraced by hundreds of millions of peoples from countries and cultures around the world.

The Umma, formed fourteen centuries ago, has experienced only two noteworthy sectarian divisions. These have given rise to the Sunni, who are the majority, and the Shi'a. The schism occurred over the problem of leadership for the Umma. The Shi'a Muslims believe that the head (*Imam*) of the Umma should be a descendant of the Prophet. They have developed a theology of the infallible Imam. On the other hand, for the Sunni Muslims, the authority of the community is based on the Shari'a which is derived from the supremacy of the Qur'an (Sunnah) and the consensus of the Umma in all matters. These two sectarian divisions do not detract from the amazing overall unity of the Muslim Umma.

Summary

The Umma is a community of Muslims who completely submit to the will of Allah and strictly follow the teachings of His Prophet, Muhammad (PBUH). The foundation of the Umma was laid by the Prophet Muhammad (PBUH) through Allah's will and mercy. The Umma transcends all tribal, national, linguistic, and racial loyalties.

A CHRISTIAN RESPONSE

Christians are impressed with the completeness of the Muslim concept of Umma, which includes a total program for social, economic, cultural, political, and religious organizations. All aspects of life are brought under the rule of the Shari'a in the Umma. This is an impressive achievement.

The Christian church also calls on peoples to bring all of life under the rule of God, a rule which Jesus the Messiah proclaimed as the kingdom of God. Nevertheless, Christians do not believe that the mechanisms of political power can establish the kingdom of God. Jesus the Messiah showed that the kingdom of God can never be politically maintained or established. When Jesus was urged by his followers to become a political leader, he refused their request. Through the Messiah, God revealed that it is in redemptive suffering love that the kingdom of God becomes present in human history.

The kingdom of God grows quietly. It is the extension of God's love and grace into human society. It is like the invisible yeast in bread, like light in darkness, or salt in food. The kingdom of God influences cultures and society from inside, but God never imposes his will on people. The kingdom of God is present whenever people open their lives to the saving grace of God.

The church, in spite of all its imperfections, is called by God to be a sign among the nations of the presence of the kingdom of God, a kingdom of righteousness and peace which transcends all national and cultural systems. It cannot be identified with any religious or political system. It has no geographical or cultural orientation. The kingdom of God is present wherever people live in a right and joyous relationship with God and their fellow human beings.

Christians should confess that we have often misunderstood the kingdom of God. We have been guilty sometimes of trying to force the kingdom of God into history. Sometimes we have tended to equate the kingdom of God with a particular national system or a particular religious culture. This we confess to be a tragic perversion of our calling as Christians, and we should repent.

Notes

1. A. A. Galwash, *The Religion of Islam*, Vol. I (Cairo: Supreme Council for Islamic Affairs, 1966), p. 94.

2. "Al-Medinah," *Shorter Encyclopaedia of Islam* (London: Luzac & Co., 1965), p. 294.

In the Name of Allah, the Compassionate, the Merciful.

9
Divine Guidance and Peace

THE MUSLIM EXPERIENCE

The Muslim desire for guidance is summarized in the opening chapter (al-Fatiha) of the Qur'an. It reads,

> Praise be to Allah, Lord of the Worlds.
> The Beneficent, the Merciful.
> Owner of the Day of Judgment,
> Thee (alone) we worship; Thee (alone) we ask for help.
> Show us the straight path,
> The path of those whom Thou hast favored;
> Not (the path) of those who earn Thine anger nor of those who go astray. (Qur'an 1:1 7)

A Muslim is the one who submits to the Divine Guidance which has been revealed by God as a mercy to humankind. In submission there is peace.

Islam is peace

Islam is the way of peace. The Muslim community, the Umma, is the community of peace which has surrendered to the will of God. Anyone can experience peace if he has unequivocal faith in the one true God-Allah and has completely surrendered to Allah's will and commandments. The submission which is peace includes the faith confession, believing in the Books of God, obedience to the Prophet, and submission to the Law of God. We shall briefly discuss each of these aspects of surrender.

The Shahada

The true believer in Islam must take the *Kalimah* or *Shahada* very seriously—"*La ilaha illa 'llah, Muhammadu rasul Allah.*" The *Shahada*, which states that there is no god worthy of worship except Allah, is the covenant of submission which God has given to humankind. It is the same covenant of submission which all prophets of Allah, from Adam to Muhammad, came to renew.

Pronouncing the Shahada must be a sincere confession of deeper understanding and appreciation for the one true God, Who is the Creator, Master, and Ruler of all that is in existence in the universe. Only He is transcendent and possesses all the Divine attributes. He is beyond and above all His creation, and to associate anyone in His worship is a grave sin. The Qur'an witnesses,

> Or assign they unto Allah partners who created the like of His creation so that the creation (which they made and His creation) seemed alike to them? Say: Allah is the Creator of all things, and He is the One, the Almighty. (Qur'an 13:16)

This one true God is also the all-loving, the all-Generous, the all-Benevolent, the all-Merciful, the Compassionate, and the most Forgiving. Peace is at the door of all believers who submit to Allah's will, obey His commands and law, and associate none with Him in their worship.

The Qur'an

As mentioned previously, God has revealed His commands by sending His Books of Divine guidance through His messengers. The Qur'an, as the last revelation, is the final criterion of truth, and all Muslims must submit to its Divine authority. The Muslim experiences peace in grateful submission to the marvelous will of God as revealed in the Qur'an.

The Sunnah

It is through the Prophets that the Oneness of Allah and His Divine Books are revealed. Therefore, the true servant of Allah must also believe in all the Prophets including the Prophet Muhammad (PBUH), the Seal of all Prophets. No one is considered a believer

unless he obeys the Prophet, through whom the Qur'an was revealed. The way of the Prophet (Sunnah) is the path of Divine
guidance. The Qur'an says,

> Those who disbelieve in Allah and His messengers, and seek to
> make distinction between Allah and His messengers. . . . Such
> are disbelievers in truth; and for disbelievers We prepare a
> shameful doom. But those who believe in Allah and His messen-
> gers and make no distinction between any of them, unto them
> Allah will give their wages; and Allah was ever Forgiving, Merci-
> ful. (Qur'an 4:150-152)

Allah demands complete obedience to Muhammad (PBUH)
and all of Allah's apostles. Since Prophets come with God's guidance, the believer has no alternative except to obey the instructions
of these Divinely guided messengers. As for the Seal of Prophets to
whom Muslims turn for instruction, the Qur'an remarks, "We have
not sent thee (O Muhammad) save as a bringer of good tidings and
a warner unto all mankind; but most of mankind know not"
(Qur'an 34:28).

The Prophet Muhammad (PBUH) told the Muslims to follow
his instructions in regard to all he received as revelation from
Allah. Muhammad's (PBUH) life was sanctioned as a model life for
all humankind. His explanation of the Qur'an was Divinely sanctioned. Muslims cannot make decisions counter to those made by
the Prophet. The religious significance of the Prophet Muhammad
(PBUH) is summarized, "Verily in the messenger of Allah ye have a
good example for him who looketh unto Allah and the Last Day,
and remembereth Allah much" (Qur'an 33:21). Therefore, sincere
belief in the Prophet and strict obedience to his teachings and example is the one sure way for a Muslim to achieve peace.

The Shari'a

The Muslim Umma, which is the community of peace, must strictly
follow God's guidance. This guidance or law is contained in both
the Qur'an and the *Sunnah* (practices) of the Prophet. This code of
Allah is also referred to as the *Shari'a*, and literally means "road" or
"path." The Shari'a is the very road, which if properly followed,

leads man to peace. The Shari'a combines the guidance contained in both the Qur'an and the Sunnah, and its very basis is the *Shahada*.

Shari'a (which will be discussed further in another chapter) is the Muslim sacred law. It is the Divine Law. It is the law to which all Muslims must subordinate all their life affairs, both public and private. Rejection of the Shari'a is a rejection of the faith of Islam. The Shari'a is the ideal pattern for a Muslim's life and the law which unites all Muslims into a single Umma. Strict observation of the Shari'a gives believers hope of happy lives in this world and the next one. The Shari'a is the course through which God has chosen to guide humans. Strict adhesion to Allah's code is the way of experiencing peace (Islam) because the Shari'a combines all aspects of Divine guidance.

Personal Ibadat

The submission which is peace is first and foremost an individual effort. Allah, the all-Merciful, the Benevolent, has given people guidance through His Prophets and Scriptures. He has done all this to help humankind submit to the only true source of guidance, Allah. Every believer must strive for submission which is peace.

Belief alone is not enough. People must practically perform all the duties required of them by the Islamic faith. They must do the *Ibadat* (devotional worship). Ibadat is a wide concept, and we have devoted a later chapter to it. Worship involves performing all the primary duties commanded by God and all other good deeds. Ibadat is the total experience of complete and unreserved submission to the will of Allah.

Muslims believe that peace is only achieved through total commitment to Islam. Specifically, we mean that peace is experienced through total commitment to the Shahada, belief in the Qur'an and Muhammad (PBUH) the Apostle of God, and total devotional submission to the Shari'a.

Those who refuse to surrender to Allah's will cannot experience peace. In fact they experience hell. Allah has said,

> I smite with My punishment whom I will, and My mercy embraceth all things, therefore I shall ordain it for those who ward off (evil) and pay the poor-due, and those who believe Our revelations. (Qur'an 7:156)

Summary

Through His mercy and justice, Allah will know whom to save from hell. There is no one to help man, except his own upright faith as ordained by Allah and His mercy. Warning man against sin, Allah proclaims,

> Say: I am (relying) on clear proof from my Lord, while ye deny Him. I have not that for which ye are impatient. The decision is for Allah only. He telleth the truth and He is the Best of Deciders. (Qur'an 6:57)

A CHRISTIAN RESPONSE

The Christian witness, like the Islamic witness, invites people into an experience of God's peace. Christians believe true peace is the experience of a right and joyous relationship with God. The Bible often speaks of "peace with God." Christians believe the true peace with God is the experience of salvation from sin. We believe that because of our sinfulness it is impossible for us adequately to fulfill all the will and commands of God. We believe our Ibadat is imperfect and inadequate. Nevertheless, Christians also believe that through Jesus, the Messiah, God has made it possible for all humankind to receive salvation and peace.

The Bible says, "For it is by grace you have been saved, through faith—and this not your own doing, it is the gift of God—not because of works lest any man should boast. For we are [God's] workmanship, created in Christ Jesus for good works, which God prepared beforehand, that we should walk in them" (Eph. 2:8-10). The Christian witness is that we receive peace and salvation by faith in what God has done for us through Jesus, the Messiah.

In the Name of Allah, the Compassionate, the Merciful.

10
Worship

THE MUSLIM PRACTICE

Worship (singular—*ibadah*, or plural—*ibadat*) is submissive obedience to one's Master, God. It is, therefore, the most profound religious practice. Ibadah is the confession that Allah is the Lord and Master, and man is the servant or slave. All that the servant does in obedience to God constitutes ibadah.

The Qur'an says,

> Lo! As for me, my Lord hath guided me unto a straight path, a right religion, the community of Abraham, the upright, who was no idolater. Say: Lo! my worship and my sacrifice and my living and my dying are for Allah, Lord of the Worlds. He hath no partner. This am I commanded, and I am first of those who surrender (unto Him). (Qur'an 6:162-164)

The concept of ibadah in Islam is comprehensive. The central point is to acknowledge wholeheartedly that only Allah, the Creator of all things, is worthy of worship. Allah has ordained some aspects of religion (*al-Din*) which constitute particular expressions of worship.

Three obligatory dimensions of Islamic worship are:

Submission to Allah (*Islam*)

Belief or faith (*iman*)

Righteousness (*ihsan*).

The attitude or spirit of right worship includes prayer (*du'a*), fear of Allah (*khawf*), hope (*raja*), trust (*tawakkul*), aspiration (*raghbah*), remorse (*inabah*), sacrifice (*dhabh*), vowing (*nadhr*), homage (*khushu*), appeal for refuge (*istiaanah*), appeal for succor (*istighathah*), supplication (*istiqanah*), awe (*rabbah*), apprehension (*khashyah*).

All these forms of worship should be directed to no one other than God. True worship is to ensure that all these practices are directly and exclusively performed for Allah. The Qur'an teaches, "He who crieth unto any other god along with Allah hath no proof thereof. His reckoning is only with his Lord. Lo! disbelievers will not be successful" (Qur'an 23:117). A worshiper must confess that God is the only reality. He is the Lord, the Creator, the most Gracious.

The right attitude in Worship (Ibadat)
First, we shall discuss several of the right attitudes of worship. Then we shall briefly discuss the obligatory rituals, beliefs and practices.

Fear is a cherished attitude in Muslim worship. The Qur'an states, "It is only the devil who would make (men) fear his partisans. Fear them not; fear Me, if ye are true believers" (Qur'an 3:175). So if you desire good and not evil, fear God in whatever you do; then you are performing true ibadah.

Hope and *trust* in God are also important in true worship. A person who puts all his hope and trust in God in all that he is doing is performing true ibadah. Such a person is raised to great spiritual dignity which is a great reward. Allah says, "Who hath created seven heavens in harmony. Thou (Muhammad) canst see no fault in the Beneficent One's creation; then look again: Canst thou see any rifts?" (Qur'an 68:3).

Remorse is another important aspect of worship that must be taken seriously by Muslims. In the Qur'an Allah advises Muslims to repent and be righteous, before it is too late and judgment is established. The Qur'an says, "Turn unto Him repentant, and surrender unto Him, before there come unto you the doom, when ye cannot be helped" (Qur'an 39:54).

Supplication is one of the most important aspects of Muslim worship. In the Qur'an we read, "Praise be to Allah, Lord of the Worlds. . . . Thee (alone) we worship; Thee (alone) we ask for help" (Qur'an 1:1-4). This means Muslims do not only worship God and ask for His help, but emphatically worship Him alone and ask for His aid only, for He is the only One worthy of devotion and able to help people. The Prophet Muhammad (PBUH) said, "If you need aid, offer supplication to Allah."[1]

It is ibadah for a Muslim to *faithfully fulfill his vows and oaths of spiritual service*, including service to humanity. If a person fulfills his vows in his commercial and economic dealings, in his contracts and in his dealings with all the people he meets, relatives, friends, or strangers, all that constitutes ibadah. The Qur'an witnesses, "They perform the vow and fear a day whereof the evil is widespreading" (Qur'an 76:7).

To seek refuge in God is yet another important aspect of worship. God is the Creator, the Sustainer, the Ruler, and the Master of the day of judgment. God is therefore the only Being entitled to man's worship at any time. It is man's duty to worship God by seeking His protection against evil. God protects those who in worship take refuge in their Lord. To this effect the Qur'an teaches, "I seek refuge in the Lord of mankind, The King of mankind" (Qur'an 114:1-2).

Sacrifice is also a significant expression of worship. As for sacrifice, the Muslim witness is quite clear. Sacrifice is not for appeasing higher powers, for God is One. God is not interested in the flesh and the blood of our sacrifices, but only as a symbol of thanksgiving to Him by sharing the flesh of the sacrificial animal with our fellowmen. It is the devotional state of the mind which is important in sacrifice. The Qur'an tells us, "Their flesh and their blood reach not Allah, but the devotion from you reacheth Him" (Qur'an 22:37). In another Qur'anic verse, we are further informed that

> Lo! my worship and my sacrifice and my living and my dying are for Allah, Lord of the Worlds. He hath no partner. This am I commanded, and I am first of those who surrender (unto Him).
> (Qur'an 6:163-164)

We have described only several aspects of the right attitudes and expressions of worship. Now we need to consider some aspects of the obligatory rituals and practices of worship.

The obligatory rituals, beliefs, and practices of ibadah

We have seen that ibadah is a means for purifying man's physical and spiritual life. We have described some required expressions or attitudes of worship. In addition to these worshipful attitudes, Allah has also commanded certain obligatory rituals, beliefs, and practices of ibadah. We have already noted that these include: (1) submission (*Islam*) with its pillars of duty; (2) faith (*iman*) with all its articles of belief; (3) good deeds (*ihsan*).

The obligatory acts or rituals of the ibadah of duty which make up submission (Islam) consist of five pillars: (1) testifying that there is no god but Allah and that Muhammad (PBUH) is His messenger; (2) performing prayers (*salat*); (3) paying obligatory alms (*zakat*); (4) fasting during the month of Ramadhan (*saum*); (5) performing the pilgrimage to the Ka'bah (*haj*).

The obligatory beliefs of ibadah which make up iman are belief in: (1) One God (Allah), (2) His angels, (3) His books, (4) His messengers, (5) the last day, (6) His power (*Qadar* and *Qatha'*).

Finally the obligatory practice of ibadah which makes up ihsan (right doing) is to worship Allah as if you are seeing Him, for though you do not see Him, He is seeing you.

It is not our intention to discuss all the obligatory rituals, beliefs, and practices of ibadah as outlined above. We are going to restrict our attention to several aspects of ihsan (right doing or righteousness) and salat (prayer), which is a very important form of the ibadah of submission (Islam), because salat is an exceedingly important pillar of duty.

Right conduct (Ihsan)
Right conduct is an obligatory form of worship. The ibadah of ihsan is absolutely essential, because every good deed performed in submission to the will of Allah is indeed an act of worship. Righteousness covers so many areas of our private and public life that we cannot exhaust it here. If a man helps the poor, gives food to the hungry, helps the sick, or performs other similar acts, not from selfish motives, but only to seek the pleasure of God—that is true worship. About righteousness the Qur'an has the following to say:

It is not righteousness that ye turn your faces to the East and the West; but righteous is he who believeth in Allah and the Last Day and the angels and the Scripture and the Prophets; and giveth his wealth, for love of Him, to kinsfolk and to orphans and the

needy and the wayfarer and to those who ask, and to set slaves
free; and observeth proper worship and payeth the poor-due.
And those who keep their treaty when they make one, and the
patient in tribulation and adversity and time of stress. Such are
they who are sincere. Such are the God-fearing. (Qur'an 2:177)

Prayer (Salat)
Salat is the fundamental and most important obligation of ibadah.
The Prophet is reported to have said, "Salat is the pillar of Religion
and whosoever abandons it, demolishes the very pillar of religion."[2] On another occasion the prophet described salat as "the essence of worship." It is through prayer that a Muslim totally and
practically submits to Allah.

Prayer is a religious duty. It is ibadah. God says, "Pray unto me
and I will hear your prayer. Lo! those who scorn My service, they
will enter hell, disgraced" (Qur'an 50:60). Salat is a fulfillment of an
obligatory duty, an act of homage toward God, a duty commanded
to all the faithful. He who willfully avoids salat forsakes Islam.

Prayer is the heart and essence of religion. Prayers will be ac-
counted for first on the day of judgment, before any other duties.
We learn from a Hadith that "Should one's prayers be marked as
perfect, all his other deeds will win the satisfaction of the Merciful
Lord."[3] Because prayer is very important, it is the first duty imposed
by God on humankind, after believing in His Oneness.

It is prescribed for a Muslim to pray five times a day—before
sunrise, between midday and afternoon, in the afternoon, immediately after sunset, between the time when twilight is over and just
before dawn. The various poses and postures the worshiper makes
in prayer are a true embodiment of the spirit of total submission to
Allah. The various recitals strengthen his commitment to the Almighty God. The frequency of the prayer is a good lesson for the
worshiper in discipline and willpower. Prayers strengthen the
foundation of one's faith and prepare him for a life of virtue, submission to Allah, inner peace, and stability. They help to guide man
to the most upright way of life—a life of sincerity, patience, courage,
confidence, and hope.

Before a Muslim presents himself before his Lord to offer
prayers, he must be spotlessly clean and pure. The Qur'an states,

"Truly Allah loves those who turn to Him and those who care for cleanliness" (Qur'an 2:222). Islam takes interest in the purification of the body from all dirt and impurities, as well as purification of the mind from false, wrong, and corrupt beliefs and attitudes. This purification of the mind, body, and clothes is called *taharah* (purification). It is only when a Muslim worshiper is in the condition of taharah that he can perform the salat. The purification of the body can be made through a partial wash of those parts of the body which are generally exposed to dirt or dust, or through a complete bath. The partial wash is better known as *wadu* (ablution), and the complete bath is called *ghusul.* All this proves the importance of salat as a form of worship.

It is recommended that prayer be performed in a mosque and in a congregation if there is one available. This is more true of the *Juma* (Friday) congregational prayer, which is compulsory to all Muslims. On all other occasions, Muslims will also prefer to pray in a mosque if one is available. But if it is not convenient to go to a mosque, Muslims may pray wherever they happen to be—at home, in the market, in parks, at a railway station, in an embassy yard, or on board ship. It is a common sight to see a Muslim praying by the roadside.

Muslims can perform salat anywhere. The Qur'an says: "And the places of worship are only for Allah." (Qur'an 72:18). Nevertheless, the common feature which Muslims all over the world must observe is standing barefooted, all facing toward Makkah (Qibla), and conducting the service in the language of the Qur'an. This universal practice of salat among all Muslims around the world distinguishes Muslims from non-Muslims. The unity of the worldwide community of Islam is evidenced in the common ritual of salat.

We have discussed salat as one aspect of the ibadah of submission. We have not discussed the other rituals of duty, nor have we probed any aspects of the ibadah of iman (belief). We have only briefly discussed the ibadah of ihsan (right doing). But salat is a key dimension of the whole experience of ibadah. As such salat reveals the inner meaning of worship in Islam. In fact, Islam is ibadah.

The essence of Islam is ibadah. It is in worship, which is a total way of life, an expression of complete and grateful submission to

God, that a Muslim gives witness to the reality of his faith in God. Through ibadah, the Muslim expresses the submission and peace which is Islam.

From what we have identified as ibadah, we assert confidently that there is no Islam without ibadah. It is through ibadah that Islam is given meaning. It is ibadah that provides the pillars of support for the edifice of Islam.

Abu Huraira reports in a Hadith that an Arab came to the Prophet and said, "Guide me to a deed by doing which I shall enter paradise."

The Prophet replied, "Worship God and do not associate anything with Him, observe the prescribed prayer, pay the obligatory *zakat* (alms), and fast during Ramadhan."

The Arab responded, "By Him in whose hand is my soul, I shall not add anything to it nor fall short of it."

When he had left, the Prophet remarked, "If anyone wishes to look at a man who will be among the people of paradise, let him look at this man."[4]

So if anyone performs all his essential obligations (ibadah), without leaving out any one of them, his place is in paradise. It is through proper worship that man can hope for paradise.

A CHRISTIAN RESPONSE

The Muslim witness in worship is profound. Right worship is a prominent Muslim concern, and many Christians who have Muslim friends are impressed by the sincerity and devotion of Muslim worship. The Muslim discipline of prayer, fasting, or almsgiving is impressive. Christians appreciate that the essence of Islamic worship is submission to God. As Christians hear and see the Muslim witness in worship, they are often challenged to also become more disciplined in their own experience of worship.

At the same time, the Christian witness invites all true worshipers of God to move beyond the mystery of the forms of worship into an actual encounter with God, a personal fellowship relationship with the one whom both Muslims and Christians worship. The forms and practices of our worship are less important than the spirit in which we worship. Jesus the Messiah invites us to worship God as our loving heavenly Father. We are invited to worship our heavenly Father in spirit and in truth. We are invited to joyously participate together in the bounty of His grace and love.

It is for this reason that eating and drinking in fellowship together in the presence of God (the communion or eucharist) is the most profound symbol and expression of Christian worship; it is a sign of God our loving heavenly Father being graciously present among His people.

As we worship in the presence of God, both Muslims and Christians are reminded that the true worship acceptable to God is a right attitude.

A MUSLIM CLARIFICATION

The fact that Muslims are very concerned about the right forms for worship should not obscure the other fact that a true Muslim should be equally concerned about having a right attitude of total submission to God in his worship. In Islamic worship, the right ritual and right attitude belong together. The third dimension of Islamic worship, ihsan, concentrates on right attitude. The Qur'an says, "It is not righteousness that ye turn your faces to the East and the West; but righteous is he who believeth in Allah" (Qur'an 2:177).

Notes

1. Al Bukhari, *Hadith*.

2. Reported by Umar, *Al-Hadith*, Vol. 111 (Lahore: The Book House by Fazul Karim, N.D.), p. 169.

3. Reported by Abi Hurayirah, *Sahih Tirmidh* (Damascus: L-lftai by Minhaji Salihin & Izudin Baliyk, N.D.), p. 134.

4. Al-Bukhari, *Hadith*.

In the Name of Allah, the Compassionate, the Merciful.

11
Right Conduct

THE MUSLIM IDEAL

The Almighty God has revealed to the Prophet Muhammad (PBUH) a Divine Law and a permanent scheme of values. These are the ideals on which Muslim conduct must be based. First, we shall discuss the Divine Law (*Shari'a*) as the basis for right conduct. Then we shall briefly describe Islamic values.

The Shari'a: what is it?

Shari'a is etymologically derived from an Arabic root, "the trodden path." It is the "path" which leads men into submission. Shari'a is the Divine Law revealed by God to the Prophet Muhammad (PBUH) for the guidance of the Muslim community. It is the detailed code of conduct for Muslims to follow, both in their private and public lives. It is a well organized system of universal law for right conduct. It is the Divine Law which binds all Muslims into a single Umma, even those living beyond the borders of the Muslim nation. This is the Shari'a. It is mainly through this universal law that Islam has been able to evolve a civilization, a complete culture, and a comprehensive world order.

What is contained in the Shari'a?

The Shari'a contains every aspect of human action, secular or spiritual. Political, economic, and social affairs are all regulated by the Shari'a. The ways and modes of worship, standards of morals and life are contained in the Shari'a. Through the Shari'a, man receives guidance on how to regulate his life in the best interests of God and himself.

He is given every detail on how to conduct his life, for example, how to deal with his neighbor, his parents, and those under him. While he is commanded to practice mercy, the Shari'a also instructs him on how to be merciful in particular instances. The Shari'a instructs man on how he should eat, receive visitors, buy and sell, slaughter animals, clean himself, sleep, go to the toilet, lead a government, practice justice, pray, and perform other acts of ibadat.

There is no distinction in Islam between private and public conduct, and the *Shari'a guides man to conduct his total life in line with the Divine Will.* Through the Shari'a, man can give religious meaning to his daily life. This Divine Law is the right and complete code of life for humanity.

As a complete code of life, the Shari'a has clearly shown what acts of life are compulsory (*faradh*), e.g., prayer; which are forbidden (*haram*), e.g., wine drinking; which are recommended (*sunnah*), e.g., extra prayers; which are discouraged (*mukrouh*), e.g., eating too much; which are indifferent (*mobah*), e.g., traveling by foot or by horse.

Sources of the Shari'a (Qur'an and Hadith)
The most important source of Divine Law is the Qur'an. As already observed, the Qur'an is the final perfect revelation. Every word contained in the Arabic Qur'an is from God. As a final revelation, it contains the final and most perfect solutions for all questions of belief and conduct. The Holy Qur'an contains the principles of all the Law. We should, however, not mistake it to be only a book of laws, for it contains other subjects besides law. It is just a very important source of Divine Law.

Although all the general principles of law are contained in the Qur'an, not all are explicitly clear in detail and application. They had to be explained and amplified. The natural interpreter for the Divine Law was the Prophet Muhammad (PBUH), through whom the Qur'an was revealed. The Qur'an says: "They only are the true believers who believe in Allah and His messenger" (Qur'an 24:62). And in another verse the Qur'an continues, "We have revealed unto thee the Remembrance that thou mayst explain to mankind that which hath been revealed for them, and that haply they may reflect" (Qur'an 16:44). So the Prophet was endowed with Divine wisdom (*hikma*) and authority to preach and explain the Qur'an, as is remarked, "The messenger hath no other charge than to convey (the message), plainly" (Qur'an 24:54). The prophet elaborated to his community how to interpret and apply the law as revealed in the Holy Qur'an.

When the prophet died, all his sayings and the instructions he had issued (hadith), and all his conduct and practices (sunnah) were preserved by those who were in his company. These were later rigorously sifted, combined, and compiled into books, e.g., *Sahih Muslim* and *Sahih Bukhari*. These books are known as the Hadith. They are a commentary and supplement to the Qur'an. The Hadith writings, which combine both sunnah and hadith, constitute the second basic source of law after the Qur'an. The prophetic Hadith (hadith and sunnah), as well as the Qur'an, are the infallible sources of law.

Over the years some Muslim scholars ('*ulama*), and especially the doctors of law (*fuqaha*), developed and systematized the Shari'a. They used both the Qur'an and the Hadith to write the volumes of law which are included in the Shari'a today. Two processes were used to determine the meaning of the Qur'an and the Hadith when writing Muslim Law. First, the doctors of law relied on the consensus of the Islamic community ('*ijima*). Secondly, they used analogical reasoning (*qiyas*). Both 'ijima and qiyas were the scholarly tools used to determine the practical application of the Qur'an and the Hadith. In this manner the Shari'a was formed. Over the years four great systems of law developed: Hanifite, Malakite, Shafiite, Hanbalite. These schools of law had different approaches to qiyas and 'ijima. But the Qur'an and the Hadith are the source (*madhab*) of Shari'a for all the schools of law.

Marriage

Marriage regulations are an example of the manner in which the Shari'a provides perfect guidance. The Shari'a gives careful guidance on every aspect of the marriage relationship. In Islam marriage is a solemn contract. Although monogamy is desirable, the moral code of Islam does permit polygamy or divorce under appropriate circumstances. The Shari'a carefully regulates every detail of the marriage contract or divorce proceedings. The rights of wives in a polygamous household are similarly defined by the Shari'a.

Polygamy has been practiced throughout human history. Islam did not ignore this practice nor leave it unregulated. Polygamy has been conditionally permitted, with a maximum of four wives. This conditional permission is not a pillar of faith nor an act of worship. The Qur'an teaches,

> Marry of the women, who seem good to you, two or three or four; and if ye fear that ye cannot do justice (to so many) then one (only) or (the captives) that your right hands possess. Thus it is more likely that ye will not do injustice. (Qur'an 4:3)

The maximum of four has been permitted provided they are treated with perfect equality in material and immaterial things, as well as in affection. Abdallah Yusuf says, "As this condition is most difficult to fulfill, I understand the recommendation to be towards monogamy."[1]

The regulations governing polygamy were not aimed at encouraging it as a necessity or rule. Abolishing it completely, however, was not practicable, so Islam took the practical step of permitting it, but with limitations.

Morals

Apart from the Shari'a, the second blueprint of the ideal for Muslim conduct is the scheme of moral teachings. Morality is such an integral part of Islam that moral values are mentioned in almost all passages of the Qur'an. We cannot discuss all in this short chapter. Some of those repeatedly mentioned are sincerity, honesty, humility, chastity, meekness, charity, politeness, love, forgiveness, goodness, courage, sympathy, justice, straightforwardness, obedience, appreciation, kindness, and steadfastness.

The dimensions of morality cover a number of aspects. These are mainly the relationship between human and God, human and human, humans and other creatures, and human and his internal self. The moral values in Islam teach people to desist from inflicting injury on their fellowmen, and also encourage them to do good to others.

The Muslim understanding of moral values can be partly summarized in the following Qur'anic verse,

Ascribe no thing as partner unto Him. (Show) kindness unto parents, and unto near kindred, and orphans, and the needy, and unto the neighbor who is of kin (unto you) and the neighbor who is not of kin, and the fellow-traveler and the wayfarer and (the slaves) whom your right hands possess. (Qur'an 4:36)

The positive morals, which encourage humankind to do good, stress that people must obey and love the One true God. People must peacefully surrender to the will of Allah. Submission to Allah's will serves as a source for strengthening moral qualities. These qualities include kindness and love to relatives, parents, neighbors, or strangers. Humans must respect the legitimate rights of others. They should be honest, fulfill all their commitments, and repent for their sins. They must work for a living.

Apart from those positive moral teachings, which instruct people to submit to the will of God and to be good to themselves and to others, there are other protective or precautionary moral values, which help people to abstain from injuring the life or the property of other human beings. Let us briefly discuss some of these moral teachings.

Chastity

A Muslim is restricted from casting unrestrained looks on strangers, and must refrain from listening to stories of lust and romance. All sexual relations out of wedlock are forbidden. The Qur'an says, "And who guard their modesty—save from their wives or the (slaves) that their right hands possess, for then they are not blameworthy . . ." (Qur'an 23:5-6).

The manner of dress in public is also regulated by Islamic moral values. The Qur'an states,

Tell the believing men to lower their gaze and be modest. That is purer for them. Lo! Allah is aware of what they do. And tell the believing women to lower their gaze and be modest, and to display of their adornment only that which is apparent.

(Qur'an 24:30-31)

This restraint (chastity) helps man to attain the highest form of moral values.

Honesty
Muslims are commanded to be honest and faithful and to care for that which is entrusted to them. The Qur'an teaches,

> Give unto orphans their wealth. Exchange not the good for the bad (in your management thereof) nor absorb their wealth into your own wealth. Lo! what would be a great sin. (Qur'an 4:2)

In another verse God says, "Give just measure and be not of those who diminish; and weigh things with an exact and right balance" (Qur'an 26:181-182). The various Qur'anic teachings help people to guard against all forms of corruption by remaining honest.

Peace
Islam means submission and peace. Peacefulness is one of the greatest moral values. Muslims are urged to live peacefully with one another. "Lo! Allah loveth the equitable. The believers are naught else than brothers" (Qur'an 49:9-10). Peacefulness means that no one inflicts injury to another person. This is what Islam strives for.

Politeness
Muslims have been commanded to be polite in all their conduct. They should avoid suspicion and vain talk. To this effect the Qur'an exhorts, "O ye who believe! Shun much suspicion; for lo! some suspicion is a crime. And spy not, neither backbite one another" (Qur'an 49:12).

Health and diet
While these four values—chastity, honesty, peace, and politeness—are meant to train humans to refrain from causing injury to others, there are other values which prevent humans from causing injury to themselves. Under these moral values, people prohibited from touching all sorts of intoxicants (Qur'an 2:219, 5:93-94); or eating the meat products of swine, wild animals with claws, all birds of prey, dead meat, reptiles, worms, and that which is not properly slaughtered (Qur'an 2:172-173; 5:4). This scheme of moral values has been ordained by Allah to help man develop his character and

personality in accord with Allah's will. These high moral values are necessary for the guidance of man along the straight path.

Summary
There is no Islam without profound moral values. It is God's Divine Law (Shari'a) and His permanent scheme of moral values which constitute the blueprint of the ideal for Muslim conduct. The two complement and supplement each other, and the Muslim ideal of right conduct cannot be fully realized in the absence of either.

A CHRISTIAN RESPONSE
How do we become righteous? Islam recognizes that rules and moral teaching are helpful in many ways. But the question remains: Are moral and civil regulations sufficient?

The biblical witness says,

Put off your old nature which belongs to your former manner of life and is corrupt through deceitful lusts, and be renewed in the spirit of your minds, and put on the new nature, created after the likeness of God in true righteousness and holiness.

(Ephesians 4:22-23)

"For no human being will be justified in His sight by works of the law, since through the law comes knowledge of sin. But now the righteousness of God has been manifested apart from law, although the law and the prophets bear witness to it, the righteousness of God through faith in Jesus Christ for all who believe."

(Romans 3:20-22)

Notes
1. Abdallah Yusuf Ali. The Holy Qur'an (Beirut: Dar al Arabia, 1968), p. 179.

In the Name of Allah, the Compassionate, the Merciful.

12
The Mission of the Umma

THE WORK OF THE UMMA

The first two revelations to Muhammad (PBUH) were commands to proclaim. At Mount Hira, God commanded the Prophet to recite in the name of His Lord Who created. By this very revelation, Muhammad (PBUH) had been called to prophethood. The second Divine command said, "O thou wrapped up in thy raiment! Keep vigil the night long . . . and chant the Qur'an in measure" (Qur'an 74:1-4). By this second Divine revelation, the Prophet was ordered to start preaching God's message. He was to proclaim publicly the name of the Lord, Allah. Through this revelation, Muhammad (PBUH) was called to be a Messenger of Allah.

The mission of the Prophet

By Allah's will and design, Muhammad's (PBUH) mission was made logical and successful. First, he was commanded to warn his near relatives, then his people, then the Arabs who were around them. These were followed by the whole of Arabia and last, but not least, the whole world. The Prophet's mission was to start from known to unknown. Allah says, "Lo! We have revealed it, a Lecture in Arabic, that ye may understand" (Qur'an 12:2). And in another verse it is stated, "And We have made (this Scripture) easy in thy language only that they may heed" (Qur'an 44:58).

Muhammad stood in Makkah and proclaimed the message from God. He warned unbelievers of the dreadful punishment after the day of judgment. He called the Makkans to submit to the will of God through preaching. The majority of the Quraish received Muhammad's message with open hostility. Muhammad and his retinue of followers were tortured and persecuted. The Almighty

Allah commanded him to restrain himself and to be patient. When the persecution of Muslims became intense, the Prophet was advised to migrate by Allah. The Qur'an says,

> And when those who disbelieve plot against thee (O Muhammad) to wound thee fatally, or to kill thee or to drive thee forth; they plot, but Allah (also) plotteth; and Allah is the best of plotters.   (Qur'an 8:30)

In Madinah, the Prophet welded his believers into a single brotherhood, the Umma. The Muslims soon discovered enemies of the Umma, from both within and without. It was at about this time that the Prophet was commanded to fight those who fought him and to restrain himself from those who did not make war with him. The Qur'an says, "And if they incline to peace, incline thou also to it, and trust in Allah. Lo! He is the Hearer, the Knower" (Qur'an 8:61). The Muslims were commanded, from the very beginning, not to start aggression or hostilities against other people. They were, however, to stand firm in resisting aggression and oppression directed against the Umma and humanity.

In promoting the mission of the Umma, Muslims are to follow the teachings and good examples of the Prophet Muhammad (PBUH). The Qur'an states, "They only are the true believers who believe in Allah and His messenger" (Qur'an 24:62). Muslims acknowledge that Muhammad (PBUH), as the last prophet of Allah, was the only prophet who fulfilled his mission in his life time. The last revelation he received before he died said, "This day have I perfected your religion for you and completed My favor unto you, and have chosen for you as religion AL-ISLAM" (Qur'an 5:4).

By the time of Muhammad's (PBUH) death, he had established the Umma of believers. He had also developed a complete model of Islam on this earth for humankind to follow. After the Prophet, the Umma took on the honored work of proclaiming the perfect message of Islam throughout the whole world.

The spread of Islam

The Qur'an and the Prophet Muhammad (PBUH) made it clear that they had a message for all humankind. In many passages, the

Qur'an calls on the children of Adam, or humankind, to accept Islam. The message of the Qur'an is universal, although the Arabs, who were near the Prophet, were the first to hear it. The Qur'an is addressed to all humanity. The Qur'an enlightens people concerning God and His purposes with man. The Qur'an is the true guide for people in this world, and it gives them glad tidings of the next world if they seek the righteous way of life.

Allah says, "This is naught else than a reminder unto creation, Unto whomsoever of you willeth to walk straight" (Qur'an 81:27-28).

In another verse Allah has described the Qur'an thus: "(This is) a Scripture which we have revealed unto thee (Muhammad) that whereby thou mayst bring forth mankind from darkness unto light . . ." (Qur'an 14:1).

From the start of his mission to the end, the Prophet never lost track of the universal nature of his mission, whether he was preaching to relations, Arabs, or the whole of humankind. This mission is Islam. Islam is total submission to the one true God, the Creator, the Sustainer and supreme Sovereign of all the worlds. Muslims are therefore charged with the noble mission of bringing the whole world to its supreme Sovereign and freeing it from servitude to any false god. The propagation of Islam to all people is a religious duty which must be undertaken by all true Muslims by following the good example of the Prophet who was sanctioned as "Mercy for all mankind."

Striving in the cause of God (jihad)

Jihad (striving) does not refer to war as an instrument to spread Islam. The allegation by some orientalists that Islam is intolerant and was propagated by the sword shows how little outsiders understand Islam and its mission. We will not be able to discuss in detail the allegations made by non-Muslims about Islam, and the counter statements by Muslims, reminding Christians of the massacres by Justinian the Byzantine Emperor (A.D. 527-562), the fearful wars of the Christian Clovis (A.D. 466-511), and the savage conduct of the Christian crusaders when they captured Jerusalem—all done in the name of Christianity. Islam, a complete way of life, makes no distinction between private and public conduct, between secular and the spiritual. It is in this line that war has not escaped Muslim legislation.

Several verses of the Qur'an mention that war is part of life as long as there is injustice and oppression in the world. The Qur'an says, "And if Allah had not repelled some men by others the earth would have been corrupted. But Allah is a Lord of Kindness to (His) creatures" (Qur'an 2:251). In another verse the Qur'an states,

> For had it not been for Allah's repelling some men by means of others, cloisters and churches and oratories and mosques wherein the name of Allah is oft mentioned, would assuredly have been pulled down. (Qur'an 22:40; see also Qur'an 2:216)

Islam in its practical teachings has recognized the inevitability of war and possesses the necessary legislation to regulate war.

Nevertheless, Islam does not condone spreading the Umma through war. Unfortunately when non-Muslims try to explain why the Muslim faith was embraced by so many people of the world in a relatively short time, the common reason given is that of the holy war or *jihad*. The term *jihad* has often confused non-Muslims and Muslims alike. What is jihad? In the Arabic language, the word jihad is not synonymous with war. Jihad means the exerting of one's utmost power in repelling an enemy. It is a striving in the cause of God.

The struggle in the cause of God is of three kinds. The first is the struggle against a visible enemy. The second is the struggle against the temptations of the devil. The third is the struggle against one's own passions. While carrying on a jihad, Muslims must strive with their time, knowledge, energy, possessions, talents, and all their resources for the cause of God. This is the true meaning of jihad, which was commanded by Allah and expounded by the Holy Prophet for the faithful to follow. It has a much broader meaning than fighting in battle.

We have already discussed when and why the Prophet was ordered to fight. We repeat that Islam has recognized fighting as lawful for only two purposes: self-defense and restoration of justice, freedom, and peace. Muslims are commanded not to start any aggression, and not to submit to any aggression or oppression from their enemies. The Qur'an teaches,

Fight in the way of Allah against those who fight against you. . . .
And fight them until persecution is no more, and religion is for
Allah. But if they desist, then let there be no hostility except
against wrongdoers. (Qur'an 2:190-193)

This is the condition of war in Islam. War is not the mission of Islam
nor the normal course for the Umma.

Islam is peace

Islam is the religion of peace. Its meaning is peace. It is the peaceful
surrender to the will and commands of God. The Muslim saluta-
tion "Assalaam Alikum" means, "May God's peace be on you." Islam strives to bring peace in the world. Islam will never act with aggression against non-Muslims who make peace with it or are even
indifferent to it. Islam does not force people to accept it, because it
is a faith that must come from the deep conviction of an individual.
The Qur'an categorically affirms this by saying, "There is no compulsion in religion. The right direction is henceforth distinct from
error" (Qur'an 2:256). The gracious mission of the Umma is to proclaim the message of Islam peacefully to all people of the world,
and to invite all humankind into the *Dar al Islam* (region of peace)
which is the Umma.

In his lifetime the Prophet Muhammad (PBUH) sent Muslim
envoys to carry the light of Islam to the rulers of the neighboring
countries. These were Hercalius the Byzantine Emperor, Chosres
the Persian Emperor, Negus of Abyssinia, and Hamza of Yemen.
The envoys were received with mixed feelings in the various capi-
tals. The worst reception was by the Persian Emperor. It was not
long before Roman and Persian military expeditions violated Muslim territory in cross-border raids. Orders were even given by the
Roman court for the Prophet's head. So through the death of the
Prophet, the Muslims had been involuntarily dragged into war by
their neighbors. The Muslims pushed the war to the logical conclusion a few decades later. In the process of defeating their enemies,
the Muslims did not persecute or force conversion on the local
populace.

It should be noted, however, that not every war Muslims have
fought has been in the cause of God. If the Muslims commit aggres-

sion for personal motives, they should know they are acting contrary to the true teachings of Islam and are inviting Allah's displeasure.

The Muslims followed Allah's command and the good example of the Holy Prophet by preaching Islam to the outside world. Teachers, merchants, mystics, scholars, and simple laymen—all participated in the noble task of proclaiming Islam throughout the whole world. One hundred years after the death of the Prophet, the name of Allah the Greatest was being praised as far as China to the east, Morrocco to the west, and France to the north. By the same time, Islam had made a meaningful presence in East Africa and North Africa. Today Islam has spread to all parts of the world. This shows how the Umma has been successful and active in peacefully preaching the perfect message of Allah.

Mission through service
Since Islam is a perfect way of life, service is another important aspect of the Islamic mission. The Prophet has said, "He is not a true believer who eats his fill while his neighbor lies hungry by his side." We have earlier remarked that if one generously helps the poor, the destitute, feeds the hungry, serves the suffering, he has indeed performed ibadah (worship). The third pillar of Islamic duty (obligatory alms) is imposed on Muslims to help the needy.

Because service is an important duty of Muslims, two Islamic organizations in Kenya, namely the Islamic Foundation and the Young Muslim Association, have set up free boarding schools and orphan homes in northeastern Kenya. These two organizations are an example of Islamic service ministries all over the world. Muslims are doing their best to fulfill the mission of the Umma through service to humanity.

The Umma and history
It is the will of God that all men submit to the right guidance revealed in the Qur'an and the Hadith as explained in the Shari'a. Any people who submit to the Shari'a are blessed. Although there is no compulsion in religion, and although God Himself recognizes the diversity of religious practices of peoples, now that the final Book from God has been revealed, it is right that all peoples re-

spond to the Muslim witness and submit to the Shari'a of Islam. In so doing people become part of the region of peace, the Umma.

Muslim scholars are not certain how extensive the Umma will become before the end of history. Some believe that before the final judgment, the Umma will spread to all nations and peoples. Others believe that in the latter years there will be an increase in unbelief. Nevertheless, according to the Hadith Muslims do believe that Jesus the Messiah will return at the close of history to establish Islam throughout the earth. Then there will be a resurrection and a final judgment in which God will determine who should go to hell and who should go to heaven. Hell is described as a place of fire and eternal punishment, and heaven is a paradise of joy and plenty. The best security against hell is for a person to submit to the religion of peace, the Umma, by obeying the Shari'a which has been revealed by God to the Prophet Muhammad (PBUH).

Despite problems the Umma has had to grapple with over the past fourteen centuries, it has been remarkably successful in its work. The mission of proclaiming Allah's perfect message throughout the world has been taken seriously. Many Muslim organizations like Rabita (World Muslim League-Mecca), Islamic Call Society (Libya), or Azhar University Mission (Cairo) continue to send missionaries to preach Islam in all parts of the earth. Islam, which has never known an ordained priesthood with an organized missionary backing, has generally been propagated by poor Muslims who have had to sacrifice every bit of their limited human and material resources to serve humanity.

Through sacrificial service and faithful preaching, the Umma will always strive to fulfill its mission of establishing God's Rule and Law on earth, after the example of Prophet Muhammad (PBUH).

A CHRISTIAN RESPONSE

Muslims believe that they have a witness to give to the world. The tremendous growth of the Umma is evidence that Muslims have given their witness very effectively.

Christians also believe that they have a witness to proclaim to the world. Both Christians and Muslims in their relationships to each other need to recognize that witness is at the heart of their faith. When Muslims live in lands which are predominantly Christian, the church needs to encourage freedom for Muslims to witness and for Christians to convert to Islam if they decide to do so. Freedom for witness and conversion is a basic God-given right.

Similarly, whenever Christians are in a minority in a land which is predominantly Muslim, the right of the Christians to witness freely concerning their faith should be assured by the Muslim majority. And Muslims should be free to become Christians if they so choose. A Christian community which cannot give free and open witness to its faith experiences great pain, for at the center of Christian faith is the compulsion and command of God to be a witness. Because human freedom is a basic God-given right, people should have the right to accept the witness they hear, whether it be a Muslim witness, a Christian witness, or the witness of any other faith.

Christians deeply appreciate the Muslim insistence that there is "no compulsion in religion." We confess that in our Christian history we have sometimes failed to live according to that ideal. We have sometimes used force to convert peoples to Christianity. We confess this sin and repent of it.

Christians also appreciate that ideally jihad in Islam is for self-protection and not aggression. However, when self-protection is exercised in such a manner as to prevent the church from being faithful to its witness in the world, this is exceedingly painful. Authentic self-protection should also include the willingness to hear the witness of those whom the Qur'an recognizes as being "closest in affection" (Qur'an 5:82) to the Muslims.

The Bible also affirms, like the Muslim Hadith, that Jesus the Messiah will return at the end of history. The Bible explains in considerable detail the meaning of the second coming of the Messiah. It would be good for Muslims and Christians to explore together the meaning and significance of the anticipated coming of the Messiah at the end of history.

PART II
THE CHRISTIAN WITNESS

O give thanks to the Lord, for he is good; for his steadfast love endures forever (1 Chronicles 16:34).

13
The Lord God Is One

THE CHRISTIAN WITNESS

Christians believe in one God. The key verse of the Torah[1] of the prophet Moses is: "The Lord our God is one Lord; and you shall love the Lord your God with all your heart, and with all your soul, and with all your might" (Deut. 6:4-5). God commanded the believers to teach these words to their children, to talk of God when they are at home and when they are on a journey, in the morning and in the evening, to tie these words on their hands or foreheads, and to write them on the doorposts of their houses (Deut. 6.6-9).

God is one

God is one and commands us to love him totally. It is the will of God that he become the focus of our entire lives. The oneness of God and the command that we should love God is the central teaching of the Torah.

More than a thousand years after the prophet Moses, Jesus Christ (the Messiah)[2] was asked, "Teacher, which commandment is the first of all?" Jesus answered, "The Lord our God, the Lord is one; and you shall love the Lord your God with all your heart, and with all your soul, and with all your mind, and with all your strength" (Mark 12:28-30).

Both the Torah of the prophet Moses and the gospel (injil) of Jesus the Messiah agree that God is one. We are commanded to love that one God. Only God has the right to command our ultimate loyalty.

What God is not

Why does God have the right to command our ultimate loyalty and love? God has this right because of who he is. But who is God? To understand God as revealed in the Bible, it is helpful to look at some negatives first. What is not true about God?

First, God is not the invention of the human mind. He is not the creation of humankind. He is not, as some psychologists suggest, a psycho-projection of the mind. According to the Bible, all the gods that humans invent are false. The Bible calls all human-made gods false gods or images (Hos. 13:2-3). The one true God cannot be created by people, because only God is the Creator.

Second, God is not in any way a part of nature. God created the world. No aspect of the universe is God; he is other than the creation. This is one reason the Bible condemns the worship of graven images. No aspect of creation is worthy of worship. Only God the Creator deserves our loyalty and worship (Exod. 20:4-6).

Third, God is not a philosophical principle. Philosophers often concern themselves with proofs that God exists. Much of Western and Eastern philosophy concerns itself with questions concerning the unifying principle behind the universe. Humans speculate about whether there is a God or not. The Bible has none of this. The God revealed in the Bible is the one who encounters us. He is known, not through human philosophy, but by what he does. It is God who takes the initiative to reveal himself to humankind. That is biblical theology.

God is active

If God is known by what he does, what has he done? We will look at this in greater depth in later chapters, but let us briefly note three important spheres of God's action.

First, God has acted as Creator. God is the origin of everything. Before creation was, God already existed. He is the originator of all that is visible and invisible. One name the Bible uses to refer to God the Creator of humankind is "Father." God the Father cares for his creation and especially for humankind. God has not abandoned the universe. He is always present to preserve and keep what he has created. God creates and preserves the universe.

Second, God has acted by revealing himself from time to time to the prophets. God guided the prophets (or their disciples) to write the revelations. In this way the Holy Scriptures were formed. The prophets sometimes gave witness that "the Spirit" came on them, and then they prophesied (Ezek. 2:2, Num. 11:26-30, Zech. 7:12). As the one who reveals his word through the mouths of prophets, God is frequently called Spirit.

Third, God has also acted in history. His acts in history were especially evident to the people of faith who participated in the biblical covenant community (Ps. 78:1-72). The Christian witness is that the most dramatic and definitive act of God in human history was the coming of the Messiah, Jesus. Through the Messiah, God revealed himself in a special way as Savior (Matt. 1:21).

God is love

In later chapters, we will discuss the Christian witness concerning Jesus the Messiah in greater depth. For the present we will only note that the breakthrough of the Messiah event into history is crucial to the Christian understanding of God as the one who loves humankind so deeply that he actually suffers when we do wrong. Through God's action in Jesus the Messiah, the Christian church recognizes in a special and marvelous way the astonishing affirmation that God loves people. That affirmation is the center of all that Christians believe and witness concerning God.

Christians believe that through God's revelation in Jesus the Messiah all the dimensions of God's revelation through nature, prophets, or history were fulfilled and enlightened. Through Jesus we recognize in a specific and special way that God's revelation to humankind is a drama of self-giving love. That is the key to understanding God as the Father who is the Creator, God as the Spirit who reveals himself through the words of prophets, and God as the Savior who acts in history (Luke 5:32). The apostle John, who was one of the disciples closest to Jesus the Messiah, says it simply and profoundly: "God is love" (1 John 4:16).

The love of God is the fountain of life and truth from which the Christian witness about God proceeds. Christians try to express in word and deed the love they have experienced. Yet they know what they say and do are not an adequate witness. How can a Christian witness truly convey the marvel, mystery, and unity of

God as Creator, Spirit, and Savior? How does one express the awareness that God loves totally, that the very essence of God is love, that even in God himself there is an ongoing, eternal fellowship of self-giving love, that the very unity of God is bound up in his eternal self-giving love? The Christian witness is that God is one because he is love. The one true God who reveals himself as Creator, Spirit, and Savior is a perfect unity of self-giving love (John 17:22).

Although the Bible does not use the term, later in the history of the church Christians began to use the word *Trinity* to try to express in human language the mystery of God's perfect unity and perfect love. Tertullian, in the early third century in North Africa, was probably the first church leader to use the term Trinity. It is now used in the church to express the biblical witness that there is only one God whose very essence is redemptive love. The concept of Trinity does not mean that there are three gods. Never! It is a simple but profound way to say that there is one true God who has revealed himself by what he has done as Creator, Savior, and Spirit. This one, true, eternal God is love. He overflows with love and gives himself in love for humankind.

God is a mystery

It is impossible to adequately express the mystery of God as Trinity. All examples of what we mean do not seem quite right. Nevertheless, Christian witness tries to interpret the mystery of God as Creator, Savior, and Spirit. Some people use the analogy of a person who is mind, body, and spirit. These three dimensions of the person are a perfect unity. Your mind, body, and spirit are united in one person, yet these three qualities of your personhood are expressed in different ways. You make things with your hands. You think through problems with your mind. Your spirit is expressed through your personality. These are three dimensions of your selfhood, one person.

Christians recognize that it is unwise to attempt to explain God. We need to remember that no analogy concerning God is exactly right. No one has seen God. He remains a mystery. Our attempts to explain God are never adequate. The term Trinity is an example of the inability of human language to adequately express the mystery of God who is one and who is love.

God in covenant

However, although God is a mystery, he is not unknown. The biblical witness is that God has made himself known to us. We have noted that God has revealed himself through his acts in history and especially his relationship with the covenant people of faith. In covenant[3] with God, we experience his redemptive love most perfectly.

God's covenant relationship with humans began at the garden of Eden when God made a covenant with Adam and Eve. He commanded them to till the garden, to care for it, and to have children. Adam and Eve broke that first covenant between God and humanity (Genesis 1:28; 3:24). Thereafter, the biblical account reveals repeated initiatives by God to renew a covenant with humankind. Noah, Abraham, Isaac, Jacob, Moses, David, and others were invited by God to participate in a covenant relationship with him.

God's covenant initiative at the time of the prophet Moses is particularly significant. In the book of Exodus of the Torah in the Bible, we read that the Hebrew people who were descendants of Abraham had become slaves of Pharaoh. God appeared to Moses in the burning bush and commanded him to deliver the Hebrews from bondage under Pharaoh. Moses was hesitant. He feared that he would be inadequate. Finally he asked God, "What is your name?" God answered, "I AM WHO I AM. Say this to the people of Israel, 'I AM has sent me to you' " (Exod. 3:13-15).

Moses obeyed God and became the leader of the Hebrew people as God delivered them from horrible slavery under Pharaoh. The story is wonderfully described in Exodus.

What is the significance of the new name God revealed to the prophet Moses at the burning bush? God had revealed himself to the prophet Abraham as Elohim or Allah, which is translated God Almighty.[4] That is the name for God used by Abraham, but to Moses, the great prophet of the Torah, God reveals himself as I AM (Exod. 6:2-3). The Hebrew term for I AM is Yahweh. What is the significance of God as Yahweh?

God as Yahweh reveals himself as the one who meets people redemptively. He invites people to participate in a saving covenant relationship with himself. He is the covenant God. After the deliverance from slavery under Pharaoh, Yahweh God himself met the entire Hebrew nation at Mount Sinai in the desert. The Torah describes how Yahweh met them in the thunder, lightning, thick clouds, fire, smoke, earthquake, and trumpet blast. The people feared and trembled before the power and holiness of Yahweh God.

God spoke from the mountain and gave them the Ten Commandments, a marvelous guide to right and joyous living. He also invited the people to become his covenant people. He promised that if they responded in faith and obedience to him, he would be their Father. He would bless them, care for them, and save them. God as Yahweh is the covenant God (Exod. 19:16-20, 26).

Yahweh is not far off and unknown. He is not indifferent to our needs. He is grieved by our sin and rebellion. He wants to save us, to forgive our sin, and to bless us with his love and grace. That is why Yahweh wants a covenant relationship with people. Because Yahweh is love, he himself takes an initiative to enter into a covenant with people. He reveals himself to us as the one who encounters us with his command and invitation to become his covenant people. People in the Christian church today are those who have responded to God's invitation to become his covenant people.

In a covenant relationship with Yahweh God, we learn that he is righteous, he is love, he is just, he is holy, and he can never accept what is evil or sinful. Because he loves us and desires to save us from evil, Yahweh God invites us into a covenant relationship with himself. We learn to know God when we respond to his covenant invitation in faith and repentance.

Summary

The witness of the Bible and the Christian church is that God who is love invites all humankind into a covenant relationship with himself. As we respond in faith to God, we learn to know him as our loving heavenly Father who saves and blesses us.

A MUSLIM RESPONSE

When Christians and Muslims talk about God, they are talking about the same God, although their witnessing concerning God may be rather different. When they speak of God, Allah, Yahweh, or Elohim, they mean the God Who is the only one, the Creator, the loving, the just, the holy, the merciful, the living and eternal, the wise and knowing. Nevertheless, the Christian witness emphasizes the self-disclosure of God (hence the "Trinity"), while in Islam it is the will and guidance of God which is revealed.

The roles of the prophet in Islam and Jesus Christ in Christianity are different, but at the same time, as messengers of the one true God, they have many things in common. The Christian witness that the most dramatic and definitive act of God in human history is the coming of the Messiah, Jesus Christ, is quite different from the Muslim view which believes deeply that the divine being is God himself, not as he is incarnated in history. God, according to Muslim witness, is absolute and transcendent.

The Christian witness of God as "Father" is also quite different from the Muslim witness. According to the true teachings of Islam, God is not to be conceived as having human form or attributes. He is united in design and existence. He is above all other attributes. Since He is one and the only one, a Muslim cannot invoke him in the name of the Father, Son, or Holy Spirit. All the divine attributes are well embedded in his perfect unity.

A CHRISTIAN CLARIFICATION

When Christians refer to God as Father, they should not think of God as being human. Christians share with Muslims the prohibition against conceiving of God in the form of an image. God as Father refers, rather, to a relationship. God as Father and humankind as sons and daughters of the heavenly Father is, from a Christian perspective, a description of covenant and fellowship relationship between God and humankind.

Notes

1. The Torah is the first five books of the Bible: Genesis, Exodus, Leviticus, Numbers, Deuteronomy. The Arabic name for Torah is *Taurat*.

2. Messiah is the Semitic term for the Greek term *Kristos* or Christ. Messiah or Christ means "The Anointed One." Because Arabic is a Semitic language, most Muslims are more familiar with the term Messiah than Christ. For this reason we shall generally refer to Christ with his Semitic title: Messiah.

3. A covenant is a solemn agreement between two or more people which should never be broken. In the Bible we learn that God invites people to enter into a covenant of blessing with himself.

4. Elohim and Allah derive from the same Semitic root: *El*.

The earth is the Lord's and the foulness of thereof, the World and those who dwell therein (Psalm 24:1).

14
The Creation

THE CHRISTIAN VIEW

"In the beginning God created the heavens and the earth" (Gen. 1:1). That is the first sentence in the Bible, the first verse of the Torah of the prophet Moses.

The Christian view of nature is based on the biblical witness concerning creation, which is recorded in Genesis, chapters one, two, and three, and which is also affirmed throughout the Bible. These first chapters of the Torah give the basic framework for all that is said thereafter concerning nature. Consequently, we will rely mostly on the first three chapters of Genesis for our discussion of the Christian view of nature.

Creation and development

We will comment on four aspects of the Creation story.

First, we read that God is the Creator. This is profound. It means that the universe belongs to God. He formed it and cares for it. We live on God's earth. Because he is continually concerned about the earth which he created, we are invited to pray to him when, for example, the rains do not fall. We are to work with him when they do fall. He has created and also cares for and preserves that which he has formed. Theologians speak of God's immanence when they consider his presence and care for creation.

As Creator, God is other than the earth. If there were no universe, God would still be present. No part of the universe or the earth is in any sense deity. Some people think that trees are deity; they worship trees. Many peoples think that mountains are deity; they pray to the mountains. Some people worship certain animals.

This is not biblical. The Bible insists that nature is in no sense deity.

This is why many of the Hebrew prophets preached against the practice of worshiping on the "top of every green hill." People associated hills with deity; they thought that on the hills they were especially in contact with God or the gods. The prophets declared that this is wrong. God, who created the universe, cannot be associated with anything he has made because he is other than creation. Theologians call this "otherness" of God transcendence. God as Creator is both immanent and transcendent.

Second, although God is other than his creation, it is a good creation. In Genesis, first chapter, we read that after each of the six steps of Creation, God said, "It was good." After creating man God said, "It was very good" (Gen. 1:31). The earth is good!

Some philosophers, such as the ancient Greeks or some modern Eastern teachers, believe that the material earth is not good. Only spirit is good. This is not the biblical view. The witness of the Bible is that the earth with humans on it is very good. It is to be enjoyed. The sunrise and the sunset; the falling rain and the times of drought; the trees and plants and grasses; the changing seasons; the stars, moon, and sun; the quiet movement of the wind; the fertile soil and the desert sands—all are good. God wants for us to enjoy his creation and give thanks for it. We read in the Scriptures that God "richly furnishes us with everything to enjoy" (1 Tim. 6:17).

Third, the earth is understandable. Genesis, chapter one, describes an orderly progression in Creation. God created in a logical step-by-step manner. God created light, sky, and earth; dry land and sea; plant life; the cycles of the day, night, and year with the various functions of the sun, moon, and stars; sea life and birds; all forms of land animals; and finally, humans. This progression is described in a six-step development; each of the six days of Creation was a preparation for the next phase. These six Creation days are signs of the orderliness of creation. It is an orderly and understandable universe.

We have observed three basic facts concerning the Christian view of nature. First, God is other than the creation. Second, it is a good creation. Third, it is an orderly and understandable creation.

Our fourth observation concerns the role of humans in creation. God placed Adam and Eve in this wonderful earth. He placed them in the garden of Eden and gave them the privilege of enjoying that garden. He said, "Behold, I have given you every plant yielding seed which is on the face of all the earth, and every tree with seed in its fruit; you shall have them for food" (Gen. 1:29). God gave specific responsibilities to Adam and Eve! They were to "subdue" the earth and have "dominion" over it (Gen. 1:28). They were expected to do much more than sleep and eat!

First, they were to have children; they were to fill the earth with people (Gen. 1:28). Second, they were to have dominion over the earth and to subdue it (Gen. 1:28). Third, humans were to till the earth and keep the garden (Gen. 2:15). Fourth, people were to name the animals (Gen. 2:19). And fifth, they were forbidden to eat of the tree of the knowledge of good and evil (Gen. 2:16-17). These commands are significant. They reveal to us God's intention for nature.

All of God's commands to Adam and Eve are secular—that is, they concern what humans are to do with the earth. The commands show us that people should use the earth for the good of humankind. They also suggest that God expects Adam and Eve to make the good earth, which God has created, better. Note that Genesis never suggests God created a perfect earth. The earth was "good." However, when humankind was created, God then said that it was "very good."

Before humans were created, the earth was good; after their creation, it was very good. This suggests two things.

1. The creation of humans contributes to making the earth become better than it was before they were created.
2. The "good" or "very good" earth was not perfect. There is the possibility of making the earth become better.

In other words, the creation of Adam and Eve and God's secular commands to them relate directly to making the earth become a better place. God invites people to participate with him in caring for the earth and making it better.

In modern terms we would say that God has commanded persons to participate in "development" and "progress." Learning better farming methods, building highways and factories and cities, discovering the causes of disease and using modern medicines to help cope with illnesses, controlling the size of the family so children have a fair chance to go to school and we can provide sufficient food for them to live healthy lives, mining the coal and ores, seeking for oil in the sea and in the deserts, raising better quality goats or camels—these are all examples of people fulfilling God's command. Through such activity, we sons and daughters of Adam and Eve subdue the earth, till the earth, trim the garden—in brief, we use the earth for the good of humans and make it a better place in which to live.

These concepts of development, progress, or having dominion over nature are based on the four theological legs of the Creation story.

1. God is other than nature.
2. Nature is understandable.
3. Nature is good.
4. Humans are to subdue nature.

These principles are the four foundation stones of the Christian approach to development. Because God is other than nature, we do not fear that a god will jump out of a tree and bite us when we chop the tree down, or that a deity will strike us with plague when we dynamite the granite rocks from a hillside. Because nature has been formed in a rational manner by God who is reliable and trustworthy, we are confident that we can understand to some extent the mysteries of how God put nature together. Scientific investigation, which studies the laws of nature, is one way people can obey the command of God to subdue and have dominion over nature. Because nature is good and man has been commanded by God to subdue the earth, we experience great joy in understanding nature and in using it for the benefit of people. These are the basic building blocks of the Christian approach to technology and economic development.

Selfishness and pride

Nevertheless, the Christian cannot stop there. The Bible also has a sober note, a serious warning. Adam and Eve were also commanded not to eat of the tree of the knowledge of good and evil. That tree in the middle of the garden of Eden was a sign of the possibility of using nature irresponsibly—that is, using the gifts of God selfishly, proudly, and without any sense of responsibility to God or to our fellow human beings.

There are many modern examples of the tree in the garden. Perhaps a farmer plows land which is on a hillside. When the rains come, there is danger of the soil washing away. The farmer might say that since the land belongs to him, it doesn't matter what happens to his soil. He will farm as he wants. He will not plow or plant in a manner that saves the soil from erosion. Consequently, after twenty years the soil has been washed away, and his farm has become useless. His children cannot use the land because he farmed irresponsibly and selfishly. He acted in a proud and independent way; now his farm is spoiled and he and his family have become poor.

The tree of the knowledge of good and evil is a sign from God that, although we are given the earth to subdue, we must live with humility. We dare not become selfish and proud and use nature in a destructive manner. We must not use all the fruit of the garden for ourselves. We must share with others the good gifts of nature.

The tree is a sign that we need to recognize God in all our efforts in development. The earth belongs to God, not to us. God has given us the earth to subdue it for the good of humankind, but we always need to recognize that the earth is a wonderful gift from God. We need to use this good earth as faithful stewards. We need to respect God's negative commands as well as his affirmative commands. Although he has commanded us to subdue the earth, we need to remember that he has commanded Adam and Eve not to eat from that one tree. That tree is a sign that we always need to recognize our dependence on God and never attempt to live independent of him.

Nevertheless, Adam and Eve did disobey God. They took the fruit from the tree of the knowledge of good and evil. By taking that fruit, they declared their independence from God. They were saying that they wanted to be like God. They wanted to use all the fruit of nature selfishly and independently of God (Gen. 3:1-7).

Because Adam and Eve rebelled against God, nature became less good than it had been. In fact God "cursed" the ground (Gen.

3:14-24). The ground produced thorns and thistles. Work, which should be a blessing, became a drudgery. From the "sweat of your face," people would make a living from the earth. The work of subduing the earth became much more difficult because humans had turned from God!

In the Bible, natural calamities such as drought often are interpreted as being a punishment or reminder from God that we need to depend on him and thank him for all the good gifts of nature. Although modern humans have made great scientific strides, we are always reminded through natural calamities that we are not in ultimate control of nature. God is Lord of nature. Our ability to control and use nature for the good of humankind is dependent on God. Although we are commanded by God to commit ourselves to economic and technological development, we need to recognize that pride and selfishness distorts and destroys. Whenever we live independent of God, our achievements become curses rather than blessings.

Summary

In summary, we have learned that Christians believe that the earth is God's good gift to humankind. People are commanded by God to use the earth responsibly for the joy and well-being of humankind, but our selfishness and pride distort and destroy true and joyous development of the earth.

A MUSLIM RESPONSE

Muslims, like Christians, do witness that God is the Creator. As Creator, he is other than creation. He is not nature; he is above and beyond his creation (transcendent). Muslims believe that God's creation is perfect

Muslims also believe that Adam was the first man to be created and God sent him to earth to be his vicegerent. A spouse, Hauwa (Eve), was created for Adam of a like nature to give him comfort. Before Adam and Hauwa were sent down to earth, Allah ordered them to live in the heavenly garden (paradise) and eat freely of all fruits of the garden. They were, however, prohibited from approaching the forbidden tree.[1] Satan lured and tempted them into eating the fruit of the forbidden tree.

Therefore, Allah expelled them from the garden. God sent them down to earth where they were given the honorable position of vicegerent of God on earth. "Get ye down, (all ye people) with enmity between yourselves. On earth will be your dwelling place and your means of livelihood for a time" (Qur'an 2:36). From this verse we can say that the Muslims witness, unlike that of Christians, is that the garden of Eden given to Adam and Eve was not on earth.

Muslims similarly do not contribute to the Christian view that God in fact "cursed" the ground (Gen. 3:14-24). All that God tells man in relation to the ground after the descent of Adam to earth is as quoted: "Therein Ye shall live and therein Ye shall die, and therein Ye shall be brought forth" (Qur'an 7:25).

A CHRISTIAN CLARIFICATION

The biblical reference to the ground being cursed following the Fall of humankind is primarily a description of broken and inappropriate relationships between humans and nature. It is noteworthy that the text referred to says that the ground is cursed "because of you" (Gen. 3:17). Certainly the exploitative and selfish use of nature by humans is a curse on nature. Elsewhere the Bible dramatically describes nature as groaning until humankind is fully redeemed from sinfulness (Rom. 8:19-23).

Notes

1. This tree is not specified in the Qur'an and is nameless. Some commentators think it was a tree of evil.

Thou hast crowned [man and woman] with glory and honor
(Hebrews 2:7b).

15
Adam and Eve

The CHRISTIAN BELIEF

Then God said, "Let us make man in our image, after our likeness; and let them have dominion over the fish of the sea, and
over the birds of the air, and over the cattle, and over all the
earth, and over every creeping thing that creeps on the earth." So
God created man in his own image, in the image of God he created him; male and female he created them. And God blessed
them. (Gen. 1:26-27)

In the next chapter we read that the Lord God breathed into
humankind "the breath of life, and man became a living being"
(Gen. 2:7).

The image and likeness of God

These are the first references to humankind in the Bible; this is the
witness of the first two chapters of the Torah of the prophet Moses.
People are created in the image and likeness of God! Humans have
living souls. God breathed into persons the breath of life. What
does this mean?

People are living souls created in the image and likeness of
God but that does not mean that they look like God or that God has
human form or characteristics; it obviously does not suggest physical likeness between God and humans. Instead it suggests a deep
spiritual reality; humans are capable of profound covenant relationships with God.

We need to hear the witness of the Bible as a whole to comprehend the reality of humans created in the image and likeness of

God. Much of the rest of the Bible is really a further development of the deep inner meaning of people created in the image and likeness of God, of persons as living souls who have received the breath of life from God. We can only touch the surface in this chapter, but we will discuss the most important dimensions to this biblical teaching.

First, note that both the man and the woman are created in the image and likeness of God (Gen. 1:27). Woman is as important as man. They are equally important and equally human. All humans, both male and female, are in the likeness of God.

Second, our God-likeness means that we can begin to understand creation. In the last chapter, we learned that humans are commanded by God to have dominion over the earth. We noticed that this includes the ability to study and understand the marvelous laws of nature. It is amazing that the human mind can begin to comprehend the complexity of the laws of genetics and heredity, or that humans can use the laws of gravity, thrust, and inertia so effectively that they can travel to the moon. These are complex achievements.

Equally significant is our ability to build homes in which to live; to plant gardens for food; or herd our cattle, taking them to the right kind of pastures so that they will give the maximum amount of milk. Humans in the likeness of God understand aspects of God's wonderful creation and also know how to use that creation to build better lives for themselves.

Third, we are cultural beings. Animals do not create culture. Animals operate by instinct or learned behavior, but people create cultures, which vary greatly. All dogs around the world bark in much the same manner, but human languages have immense diversity. Language is one significant aspect of culture created by human society. Similarly people live in a vast variety of houses, they create a tremendous diversity of clothing, and cook thousands of different foods. Nature shows us that God also creates enormous variety! Notice, for example, no human is identical to another human. Our cultural creativity is a dimension of our God-likeness.

Fourth, we know right from wrong. Humans are moral beings; we do not operate primarily by instinct like the animals do. The sense of right and wrong is embedded deeply in our consciences. Even though human cultures vary greatly, everywhere there is a deep sense of right and wrong. For example, although specific cultural expressions are different, people everywhere seem to sense that it is not right to kill a fellow human being. This moral consciousness is a significant aspect of our being created in the image of God.

Fifth, we sense that we should grow to become better persons. People in all cultures seem to have an awareness that they are not as good, or shall we say as human, as they should be. This is the witness of our God-likeness in our conscience. It is a persistent voice in the conscience that we should become better people, that we do not always do what we know we should do, that we really should be more kind, brave, true, reliable—more God-like. Conscience, that voice which calls us to do better, is the stamp of the image of God deep in our spirits. It is a call to grow, to become better people.

Sixth, human societies everywhere have a sense that humans are immortal. We know that death is not the end of personal existence; there is life beyond the grave. This is a significant aspect of our being created in the image of God. God is eternal. In a similar manner, God has graciously determined that we shall not vanish when our bodies die. God has determined that people, whom he has created in his own image and likeness, shall experience eternity and immortality. We shall say more about this in a later chapter.

Seventh, the image of God means that we can have fellowship with our fellow human beings and with God. Speech is important in the experience of fellowship; it is evidence that we are persons and that we long to relate to others in a deep and personal way. God also desires to have fellowship with us. God cannot have fellowship with animals because they are not people; they are not created in the image of God. People are different; they are fellowship creatures. They are humans. They are created in the image and likeness of God.

The first chapters of Genesis describe Adam and Eve as having blessed fellowship with God. God spoke with them. He conversed with them in the cool of the evening. This is God's intention for people. He desires to relate to humans in joyous and personal fellowship. That is why God invites us into a covenant relationship. The covenant between God and persons is a fellowship relationship which the Bible says is similar to that between a father and his children. In fact, that is the central aspect of being created in the image and likeness of God. We are God's beloved children; God is our heavenly Father (Deut. 32:6; Ps. 103:13; Jer. 31:9; Rom. 8:14, 17).

The Bible teaches that we find our truest humanity in a deep and meaningful covenant relationship with God. We are truly human when we live in a right and joyous relationship with God. When our loyalty and love for God is eroded, when we turn away from God and devote our lives to false gods, when we begin to live independent of God, then our humanity is distorted and spoiled.

Marriage is a sign of covenant fellowship with God. In Genesis, chapter two, we read that after God created Eve out of a rib from Adam's side, Adam joyously accepted her as his wife and said, "This at last is bone of my bone and flesh of my flesh; she shall be called Woman because she was taken out of Man." The account goes on to say, "Therefore a man leaves his father and his mother and cleaves to his wife, and they become one flesh. And the man and his wife were both naked, and were not ashamed" (Gen. 2:23-25).

For this reason, Christians do not accept polygamy as God's ideal form of marriage. In this first account of marriage in the Bible, we read that in marriage the man and the woman become one flesh. When a person has more than one spouse, loyalties are divided. Divided loyalty distorts and spoils the one-flesh unity which God intends between a man and a woman.

In much the same manner, when we give our ultimate loyalty to any authority other than God, our relationship with God is then distorted and spoiled. True fellowship with God involves total commitment to him, just as true fellowship in marriage demands total and exclusive commitment to one's marriage partner in (Hos. 2:14—3:5).

The sin of humanity

Tragically, Adam and Eve did not continue to give God their first loyalty. They turned away from God. They listened to the voice of the serpent, who is a sign of Satan. They took and ate fruit from the tree of the knowledge of good and evil, which God had strictly forbidden. By eating that fruit, Adam and Eve declared their independence from God. The Bible says they took the fruit because they wanted to be "like God." That is rebellion. It is a declaration of pride and selfishness (Gen. 3:1-7).

The witness of the Bible is that this act of rebellion by our first parents seriously and tragically distorted and spoiled the humanity created in the image of God. Although hints of the image of God remain, humankind has collectively turned away from God, and sinfulness pervades us individually and collectively. Our sinfulness is a cancer which destroys (Rom. 3:23).

Humankind's rebellion against God began at the origin of human history. Adam and Eve, the first parents of all humankind, turned away from God; they broke God's wonderful covenant with them. That very evening, after they took the fruit from the tree, God appeared in the garden to speak with Adam and Eve, but they were hiding behind the bushes, afraid and ashamed. God called, "Adam, where are you?" Adam replied, "I heard the sound of thee in the garden, and I was afraid, because I was naked; and I hid myself" (Gen. 3:9-10).

God did not leave Adam and Eve. Rather, Adam and Eve hid from God. God did not break his covenant with them. They broke their covenant with God.

God never leaves us. Because he is love, he always seeks for us and invites us to become his covenant people. It is we who turn away from him and refuse to accept his invitation to become his people. This is the story of human history—the story of humankind rejecting God, turning away from him, rejecting his wonderful invitation to become part of his covenant community of faith!

This gives two pictures of humankind. On the one hand, we are created in the image of God and are invited to participate in a marvelous covenant fellowship with God. On the other hand, we have turned away from God. The human race as a whole is in rebellion against God. We more easily do what is evil than what is good.

In the next chapter, we will say more about the Christian understanding of evil and the way it pervades human society. Then we shall also look at the biblical witness concerning God's wonderful plan to save humankind from sin, and the way God graciously attempts to recreate in us the image of God which has been spoiled by our turning away from our heavenly Father.

A MUSLIM RESPONSE

The Christian witness, that humans are created in the "image and likeness of God," is not the same as the Muslim witness. Although God breathed into humans his spirit, as both Christians and Muslims believe, for Islam the only divine qualities entrusted to humans as a result of God's breath were those of knowledge, will, and power of action. If people use these divine qualities rightly in understanding God and following his law strictly, then they have nothing to fear in the present or the future, and no sorrow for the past.

Islam further teaches that humankind is not only made in the best form of all creation, but has been made God's khalifa (vicegerent) on earth. This dignity is the natural right of both male and female and of all people regardless of race, language, or culture. The dignity of man is the supreme privilege of being the servants or slaves of Allah. It is in total submission to the will of Allah that the dignity of humankind is most fully evident. Allah says, "Surely We created man of the best stature, then we reduced him to the lowest of the low, save those who believe and do good works and theirs is a reward unfailing" (Qur'an 95:4-6).

The Christian witness that the rebellion by our first parents has tragically distorted man, and that sinfulness pervades us individually and collectively, is very much contrary to Islamic witness. Islam teaches that the first phase of life on earth did not begin in sin and rebellion against Allah. Although Adam disobeyed Allah, he repented and was forgiven and even given guidance for humankind. Man is not born a sinner, and the doctrine of the sinfulness of man has no basis in Islam.

However, despite a different conception of man in Christianity and Islam, they both believe that man needs revelation. In Islam the revelation consists of divine guidance for man, whereas in Christianity, the central concern of revelation is redemption from sin.

The heart is deceitful above all things, and desperately corrupt; who can understand it? (Jeremiah 17:9).

16
Sin and Evil

THE CHRISTIAN VIEW

Evil does not come from God, who is the righteous Creator. Evil does not spring naturally out of the good earth which God has created. It has nothing to do with the material aspects of creation, as the ancient Greek philosophers believed. They thought spirit was good and material evil. For them evil was bound up in the material or body-like aspects of creation. The Bible rejects all such notions of the origin of evil. Furthermore, evil is not caused by ignorance. Knowledge in itself is not necessarily good, nor is ignorance necessarily bad. Neither God nor his good creation is the cause of evil.

According to the Bible, we become evil when we turn away from God. Before Adam and Eve sinned, they did not experience evil, but when they took the fruit from the tree of the knowledge of good and evil, they immediately began to experience something seriously wrong in themselves, in their relationships with each other, in their relationship with God, and the good earth that God had created for them to enjoy.

In the last chapter, we said that taking the fruit from the tree of the knowledge of good and evil was a declaration of independence from God. It was an expression of pride: Adam and Eve wanted to be "like God" (Gen. 3:4). It was also a selfish act; they wanted all the fruit of the garden for themselves (Gen. 3:6). It was disobedience. God had commanded them not to eat of that one tree (Gen. 3:11).

Adam and Eve themselves decided to turn away from God (Gen. 3:1-7). It is true that Satan was present in the form of a serpent. Satan tempted them to eat the fruit, but he was not the central figure in the drama. Man and woman were at the center of the rebellion against God. They listened to the serpent's temptation and took the fruit. They reached out their own hands to take the fruit from the tree. It was their personal decision to sin against God.

Sin enters the world through the misuse of human freedom. All of us participate in the sin of humankind; all of us have misused our freedom. The Bible says, "All we like sheep have gone astray; we have turned every one to his own way" (Isa. 53:6a). We are personally and collectively responsible.

At the beginning of human history, humankind turned away from God. We should not blame Adam and Eve or our own parents for our sinfulness. All of us have personally experienced the meaning of rebellion against God. When we reflect on the story of Adam and Eve, we are really reflecting on our own personal stories as well. Each of us has fallen "short of the glory of God" (Rom. 3:23). The tragic consequences of this rebellion are described in Genesis, chapters three and four. The story of Adam and Eve is the story of each of us. It is the story of history, the story of humanity. Here are some of the consequences of sin, for Adam and Eve and for each of us.

First, Adam and Eve became ashamed of themselves (Gen. 3:7). Before they turned against God, they were not ashamed in each other's presence. They did not wear clothing. They had a beautiful and shameless relationship with each other, but after they disobeyed God, they began to try to hide themselves. They sewed fig leaves together as aprons to cover themselves. They hid behind the bushes in the garden. They were ashamed. We also try to cover our true selves with the fashionable clothing we wear or the smiles on our faces. We try to pretend that we are different from what we really are. We are ashamed of our true selves, and so we pretend. We become insincere. Shame, pretense, and insincerity are consequences of our sin. They are hypocrisy!

Second, Adam and Eve were afraid. They hid behind the bushes in the garden. They were afraid of each other, and they were also afraid of God. When God appeared in the garden as usual to have fellowship with the man and the woman, they were hiding from God. They were crouching behind the bushes hoping that God could not find them there. God called, "Where are you?"

Adam answered, "I heard the sound of thee in the garden, and I was afraid, because I was naked, and I hid myself" (Gen. 3:9-10).

Man and woman afraid of God! Hiding behind the bushes! Humans created in the image of God, humans whose greatest joy should be right and joyous fellowship with the Creator, were hiding from God, their loving heavenly Father. Humans separated themselves from God, turned away from God, hid behind the bushes. Adam and Eve, son and daughter of God, alienated themselves from their heavenly Father. Instead of loving God, they feared him! Instead of having fellowship with God, they ran to hide from God!

Third, Adam and Eve did not accept blame for what they had done; they made excuses for their sin.

God asked Adam, "Have you eaten of the tree which I commanded you not to eat?"

Adam answered, "The woman whom thou gavest to be with me, she gave me fruit of the tree, and I ate."

Then Eve said, "The serpent beguiled me, and I ate" (Gen. 3:11-13).

Adam blamed Eve for his sin. Indirectly he also blamed God. He said that it was the woman God gave him who caused him to sin. Eve, of course, blamed Satan. Neither accepted personal blame. They made excuses for their sin.

We are like that. When we know that we have done wrong, we blame others. Sometimes we blame God for our sin. Perhaps we say that because God is sovereign and all powerful, sin is really the fault of God. We may think that God should not have permitted a temptation to come into our lives. We might even become bitter against God for a certain temptation or misfortune which we experience. More often we blame Satan for our sin. "He is the one who caused us to sin," we say. Frequently we blame our parents or brothers and sisters for our failures. This common human experience of blaming others for the evil that we do is called projection of guilt by modern psychologists. We wrongly blame others for the evil *we* do.

Fourth, the marriage relationship was spoiled. Before they sinned, Adam and his wife had a beautiful relationship, but after they sinned, they began to hide their true selves from each other.

We also read that Adam began to dominate his wife, and she submitted to him (Gen. 3:16). This kind of relationship in marriage is a form of exploitation. The husband rules, and the wife submits. Because of man's rebellion against God, sex became exploitative. Women dress and act in ways that attract men. Men, on the other hand, are aggressive and try to get women to submit to them in marriage, and outside of marriage

The experience of childbirth became more painful (Gen. 3:16). Children should be a great blessing in any home, but sin brought pain into the experience of having children. Children are born through pain; they also cause their parents pain through disobedience and rebellion.

Fifth, work became a drudgery for humankind (Gen. 3:17-19). Before people turned from God, work was a blessing; it was central to the covenant God made with Adam and Eve. God commanded them to work to make the earth better. After they rebelled against God, their relationship with nature, became difficult. They began to exploit nature and the earth groaned under the exploitation. The ground was cursed because of humanity. Thistles began to grow on the land which people cultivated for crops. Humans became unkind to nature, and similarly nature became unkind to them. Humans began to struggle and fight with nature; they needed to work for their living.

Sixth, death came. God is the life-giver. We experience life when we live in a joyous relationship with God, the eternal giver of life. When Adam and Eve turned away from God, when they declared their independence from God, they were really declaring independence from the life-giver. By turning from God, they were actually turning toward death. We die because we live in rebellion against God. The Bible says "the wages of sin is death" (Rom. 6:23).

Death in the biblical sense is far more serious than biological death. Obviously a human who has the body of a creature, does experience bodily death. Biological death might be an aspect of the consequence of sin, but it is certainly not the central meaning of death as a result of turning away from God. The deeper meaning of death is the tragic spoiling of humanity created in the image of God. Our lives should reflect the glory and righteousness of God. Instead we are selfish and proud. Our humanity is spoiled. We hate instead of love. We exploit instead of share. We become bitter instead of forgiving. We become small instead of great. We become like Satan rather than like God. We are deceitful rather than truthful. We go further and further away from God; we experience death throughout our being. Death is eternal separation from God! Separation from God is the ultimate evil. Separation from God is death.

Seventh, death spreads and poisons the whole human family and all human relationships. In the family of Adam and Eve, death reigned. Cain, the eldest son, murdered Abel, the second born (Gen. 4:1-16). Cain murdered his brother because he was jealous of him. The first human family experienced murder. The elder son killed his younger brother!

That murder in the first human family was a sign that sin had spread beyond Adam and Eve. Their children also rebelled against God. In fact, rebellion against God has spread throughout the human race. Everyone everywhere shares in the rebellion against God. The Bible says, "None is righteous, no, not one" (Rom. 3:10). Again we read, "in Adam all die" (1 Cor. 15:22). The prophet Isaiah writes, "All we like sheep have gone astray; we have turned every one to his own way" (Isaiah 53:6). Each of us individually, as well as all of human society, shares in the experience of rebellion against God and death. Our common humanity is tragically spoiled. Humans as children of God, created in the image of God, have turned against God. We are sinful rather than righteous; we die rather than live.

Our sin is rebellion. It is more than the wrong acts which we sometimes do. It is we ourselves who are sinful; our hearts are evil. The Bible says, "The heart is deceitful above all things, and desperately corrupt; who can understand it?" (Jer. 17:9). The wrong things we do are a consequence of our evil hearts. We ourselves are sinful. That is why we do wrong.

The Bible describes the astonishing ways humans throughout history have experienced sin and death. Even the priest Aaron helped the people of the covenant form a golden calf which they worshiped (Exod. 32)! King David committed adultery and arranged for the murder of the good husband of the woman with whom he had sinned (2 Sam. 11). Even the prophets experience sin! The Bible is absolutely honest. Adam, Noah, Abraham, Moses,

Aaron, David—all these men of God described in the Bible experienced failure and sin. The Bible reveals that often those who seem righteous are really hypocrites and insincere. The Bible says, "All have sinned!"

History is also evidence of our sinfulness. All our history books from every culture and civilization are the stories of wars. History is the story of death: human killing human; destruction of the good things which humankind has built; the rise and fall of empires; the death of civilization; the death of empires; the death of people through wars and conflict. Humanity has fallen into death. We have turned away from God. Death is our common experience.

Rebellion against God extends beyond the human family into the world of spirits and angels. These spiritual beings are also personal and have free will. They can turn against God if they wish. Satan is an angel who rebelled. He became proud and turned against God (Isa. 14:12-14). Other angels followed his example. These evil angels obey the command of Satan who is called "the prince of the power of the air, the spirit . . . of disobedience" (Eph. 2:2). Satan and the evil angels and spirits which he leads are in total rebellion against God. They seek to destroy all that is good. The Bible calls these evil forces "the spiritual hosts of wickedness in heavenly places" (Eph. 6:12). These evil spiritual powers are death-oriented. They attempt to bind people and societies in death.

Whether evil comes through spiritual and unseen powers or through human sinfulness, it is always the consequence of rebellion against God, the righteous life-giver. All forms of rebellion against God are evil. To live in a right and joyous relationship with God is always good, but humankind has disobeyed God. For this reason we experience death.

Summary

Our problem is this: How can we be saved from death? How can we who have turned away from God begin to experience again the joy of life? How can the image of God which has been spoiled through rebellion be recreated? The Bible is about the answer to those questions.

A MUSLIM RESPONSE

While Muslims agree with the Christian witness that Adam and Eve disobeyed God by eating the fruit of the forbidden tree, the events that followed are related differently by the two faiths. According to the Christian view, when Adam and Eve took the fruit, they were declaring their independence from God and wanted to become like God.

The Muslim belief is that Adam and Eve, having realized their mistake or sin, prayed to God for forgiveness and were pardoned. Adam was also made the first messenger of God on earth. The Christian witness minimizes the role of Satan and apportions the blame of the rebellion on man himself. Our submission is that Satan, the power of evil, was central in the whole drama and was very responsible for Adam's fall from the garden.

As Muslims, we do not accuse Adam and Eve of transmitting sin and evil to the whole of mankind. The two were absolved of their sin, and their descendants were made immune from its effect. Sin is not original, hereditary, or inevitable. It is not from God. It is acquirable through choice, but also avoidable through knowledge and true guidance from God. Muslims believe that man is fundamentally a good and dignified creature. He is not a fallen being. Muslims certainly would not agree that even prophets have participated in sinfulness!

A CHRISTIAN CLARIFICATION

While it is true that some Christian theologians have often spoken of concepts such as original sin or hereditary sinfulness, these specific terms do not adequately explain the collective and personal sinfulness of humankind of which the Bible speaks. From a biblical perspective, it is far more important to recognize that we need redemption from our sinfulness than it is to develop theories as to precisely how sin is or is not transmitted.

Thy word as a lamp to my feet and a light to my path (Psalm 119:105).

17
The Word of God

WHAT ARE THE CHRISTIAN SCRIPTURES?

Christians believe that the Bible is the written Word of God; it is inspired by God. The witness of the Bible concerning itself is that

> All scripture is inspired by God and is profitable for teaching, for reproof, for correction, and for training in righteousness, that the man of God may be complete, equipped for every good work.
> (2 Tim. 3:16-17)

The word *inspire* means to breathe. Christians believe that the Holy Scriptures have been "breathed" by God. The thoughts of God were breathed into the holy persons of God who spoke or wrote God's Word. The Bible has been inspired by God.

Divine inspiration does not mean divine dictation. Christians do not believe that the prophets who spoke or wrote the Word of God were tubes through which God's words flowed. In all of the biblical Scriptures, the personality of the different writers is evident. The prophet David wrote as an inspired poet; he was a poet. The prophet Jeremiah spoke as an inspired preacher; he was a preacher. The gifts and personalities of the writers are part of the scriptural message. God's inspiring activity did not cancel human involvement in the process; the imprint of human personality is part of the content of biblical revelation. The Bible is the marvelous drama of God revealing himself to persons, and the inspired prophets of God expressing that revelation in human language and thought forms.

The organization of the Bible

The Bible is divided into two major parts: the Old Testament and the New Testament. Testament means a covenant or a sacred promise which should not be broken. The Old Testament, or old covenant, refers to the covenant which God made with the people of Israel at Mount Sinai after he had delivered them from slavery under the Pharaoh. At Mount Sinai, God gave the people of Israel the Ten Commandments (Exod. 20:1-17). He invited them to become his covenant people and promised to care for them as a father for his children. The Old Testament is the record of God's revelation of himself and the response of the people of faith to become his covenant people.

Tragically, the people of Israel failed to trust in God as they should have. Even when they were still at Mount Sinai, they began to worship a golden calf. Repeatedly they turned from God. They were not able, and often not willing, to obey the good commands of God. They were a sinful people (Exod. 32:7-10). Slowly God led the prophets of the Old Testament to realize that the old covenant was not adequate. They came to recognize that God would make a new covenant with humankind, a covenant of power and grace that would transform the inner heart of humankind, a covenant that would recreate the image of God in humans — the image spoiled so tragically through rebellion against God.

The prophet Jeremiah speaks of the new covenant in this way:

> Behold, the days are coming, says the Lord, when I will make a new covenant with the house of Israel. . . . I will put my law within them, and I will write it upon their hearts; and I will be their God, and they shall be my people. (Jer. 31:31, 33)

The prophets of the Old Testament also recognized that the new covenant would be fulfilled through the Messiah. In fact, when Adam and Eve sinned, God revealed that a child born to the woman would crush the head of evil (Gen. 3:15). Although this is the first prophecy in the Bible concerning the Messiah, the prophetic development throughout the Old Testament increasingly anticipated that the promises of God to humankind would be fulfilled and completed in the Messiah. He was the one through whom God would create a new and better covenant with humankind (Isaiah 11:1-9).

The Old Testament prophecies concerning the Messiah were amazingly specific. Here are a few examples.

He would be from King David's family (2 Sam. 7:12-13).
He would be born of a virgin (Isa. 7:14).
He would be born in Bethlehem (Mic. 5:2).
He would be "God with us" (Isa. 7:14).
He would not be accepted by humankind (Isa. 53:3-9).
He would suffer and die with the wicked (Ps. 22:16-17).
He would be buried in a rich man's grave (Isa. 53:9).
He would rise from the dead (Ps. 16:10).

These are only a few of the many Old Testament prophecies about the coming Messiah, all of which were fulfilled by Jesus.

The New Testament is the record of the way God fulfilled the Old Testament (old covenant) prophecies concerning the Messiah and established the new covenant. It contains the account of the life and teachings of the Messiah and the creation of the church which is the new covenant community. The Old Testament anticipates the coming of the Messiah. The New Testament reveals that the Messiah has come.

We need both the Old and the New Testaments to understand and accept God's revelation to humankind. The Old Testament is a preparation for the New Testament; the old is a sign of the new; the new fulfills the old. Christians accept both testaments as God's inspired written Word.

Now we need to look more closely at the contents of these two parts of the Bible.

The Old Testament

The teachings and writings of about thirty prophets are included in the Old Testament. God's revelation through some of the prophets is so significant that whole sections of the Old Testament are named after particular prophets. For example, the revelation of God through the prophet Jeremiah is recorded in the book of the Old Testament called Jeremiah. Some portions of the Old Testament mostly concern the history of the covenant people. Other parts are the songs and hymns which were chanted by the people in worship. These different types of Scripture have been divided into three main divisions in the Old Testament: the Torah, the Prophets, the Writings. We will comment on each of these major parts of the Old Testament Scriptures.

The Torah (Taurat) of the prophet Moses is the first part of the Old Testament. It contains the first six books of the Bible—Genesis, Exodus, Leviticus, Numbers, Deuteronomy, and Joshua. Moses is the great prophet of the Torah and in fact of the entire Old Testament. In the Torah we read that God specifically commanded Moses to write the words of the covenant (Exod. 34:27-28). This is unusual. Usually in the Old Testament the prophet "saw" or "heard" the Word of the Lord, which he proclaimed to the people. Faithful disciples or scribes then wrote the Word of God which had been revealed through the prophet (for example, note Jer. 36:4). However, we read that Moses himself wrote portions of God's revelation with his own hand (Deut. 31:9). We are confident that the Torah as a whole has come to us through the prophet Moses and his faithful disciples, who preserved and transmitted these inspired revelations so we can read them today.[1]

The second part of the Old Testament is the Writings. The Writings include books on the history of the covenant people and books of poetry. The history books are Judges, Ruth, 1 and 2 Samuel, 1 and 2 Kings, 1 and 2 Chronicles, Ezra, Nehemiah, and Esther. The books of poetry are Job, Psalms, Proverbs, Song of Solomon, and Ecclesiastes. Of these five books of poetry, the best known is the Psalms. Muslims call the Psalms the Zabur of the prophet David. Certainly David did write many of these psalms. Many psalms are beautiful hymns of praise to God for his great love and mercy to humankind.

The third portion of the Old Testament is the Prophets. These books are Isaiah, Jeremiah, Lamentations, Ezekiel, Daniel, Hosea, Joel, Amos, Obadiah, Jonah, Micah, Nahum, Habakkuk, Zephaniah, Haggai, Zechariah, and Malachi. In a sense all of the writings of the Old Testament are prophetic. However, whenever the faith of the people of the covenant seemed to be in decline, God sent prophets to call the people back to himself. All of the prophets commanded the people to repent and to return the covenant God had established with them at Mount Sinai when he revealed the Ten Commandments through the prophet Moses. At the same time, the prophets began to recognize that the old covenant was not good enough. They looked forward to the coming of the Messiah, whose life and teachings are recorded in the New Testament.

One of the greatest Old Testament prophets was Isaiah, who foresaw in a marvelous way that the Messiah would establish a new covenant which would be a blessing to all humankind. He also prophesied that the Messiah would suffer and give his life for the sins of the people.

The New Testament

The first four books of the New Testament are known as the gospel or the injil.[2] Christians believe that the Messiah himself is the gospel. We shall say more about this in a later chapter, but for now it is important to recognize that the gospel is the record of the life and teachings of Jesus the Messiah. It consists of both his life and his teachings, because he himself is the gospel. The revelations through what the Messiah is and does are just as significant revelation through what he taught and proclaimed. Consequently, the written gospel is a presentation of the Messiah.

The gospel, who is the Messiah, was seen by people. Those who were the closest to the Messiah were called disciples. Some of these disciples became apostles of God. These apostles were witnesses of the gospel. They had lived and been with the Messiah. They knew him personally. After the death and resurrection of the Messiah, God inspired the apostles to record what they had seen and heard. The records of Matthew, Mark, Luke, and John have been written in four books. Each book is an apostolic witness concerning Jesus the Messiah. The witness aspect of these gospel Scriptures is beautifully affirmed in the opening verses of the gospel as recorded by Luke.

> Inasmuch as many have undertaken to compile a narrative of the things which have been accomplished among us, just as they were delivered to us by those who from the beginning were eyewitnesses and ministers of the word, it seemed good to me

also, having followed all things closely for some time past, to write an orderly account for you, most excellent Theophilus, that you may know the truth concerning the things of which you have been informed. (Luke 1:1-4)

The gospel witness has been recorded through the inspiration of God so that we "may know the truth" (Luke 1:4).

The New Testament includes much more than the record of the life and teachings of Jesus Christ. The fifth book of the New Testament is called the Acts of the Apostles. This book is a brief history of the apostolic church. It tells how the new covenant community was formed and describes the way in which the people of the new covenant carried forward their mission in the world, continuing the work which Jesus the Messiah had begun. Acts includes a number of sermons by apostles. These messages reveal the basic meaning of the life, death, and resurrection of Jesus the Messiah. The Acts of the Apostles is the earliest history of the church.

Then come the Epistles. These are letters written by apostles or apostolic men, who interpreted the meaning of the gospel. They are Romans, 1 and 2 Corinthians; Galatians; Ephesians; Philippians; Colossians; 1 and 2 Thessalonians; 1 and 2 Timothy; Titus; Philemon; Hebrews; James; 1 and 2 Peter; 1, 2, and 3 John; Jude; and Revelation. Some of these letters were written to particular groups of Christians, giving advice and teaching concerning problems which had developed in the churches; others were written to church leaders.

For example, Philippians was written by the apostle Paul to the church in Philippi in Macedonia. The epistle to the Hebrews describes the Messiah as the marvelous fulfillment of the Old Testament. It interprets the sacrificial offerings of animals as a sign of the sacrificial death and resurrection of Jesus the Messiah. A letter by James describes the way Christians should live. All these letters to churches explain Christian belief and conduct.

Other letters were written to church leaders to teach them in how to lead the church. For example, there are two letters written by the apostle Paul to a young bishop named Timothy. Another interesting little letter, Philemon, was written to a slave master, instructing him to love his slave like a brother. Probably the master freed his slave after getting that letter from an apostle of God! The last book of the New Testament is the Revelation; it is a heavenly description of the triumph of the glorified Messiah at the end of history when God's purpose for humankind is fulfilled.

The Bible is a marvelous book. The teachings of more than thirty prophets and apostles are recorded in the Bible. The writings of the biblical Scriptures span more than a thousand years. They were written in times of tremendous change and diversity. Yet a common thread unites all these writings: God is at work in history. His intention is to redeem and save humankind from death. His redemptive activity is fulfilled and consummated in Jesus the Messiah.

Manuscripts and translations

For well over a thousand years, all biblical manuscripts were copied by hand. When a manuscript is copied, there is always the possibility of variations accidentally creeping into the text because of human error. In the late fifteenth century, Bibles were printed; this eliminated the possibility of some manuscript errors. Nevertheless, biblical scholars are concerned that our present printed texts be free of variations from the original text. To achieve this, they compare our present printed texts with the most ancient hand-copied texts available.

Biblical scholars try to make the text of the Bible we have today an accurate translation of the original. The first Old Testament was written in Hebrew, and the New Testament was written in Greek. Scholars want to know that our present Hebrew and Greek texts are reliable. They use the most sophisticated textual, linguistic, and archaeological tools to accomplish their task.

In recent years several astonishing discoveries of ancient manuscripts have greatly enhanced textual studies. For example, the 1947 discovery of the Dead Sea Scrolls at Qumran near the Dead Sea has given scholars access to manuscripts of the Old Testament which date from the second century B.C. Likewise New Testament studies have been helped by several discoveries of ancient manuscripts; one takes us to within one hundred years of the crucifixion of Jesus. There are now at least five thousand ancient New Testament manuscripts available for scholarly analysis. These studies of the ancient texts have greatly increased confidence in the accuracy of the Bible as we have it today. For example, scholars assure us that the possibility of any variation from the original New Testament text is now only one to a thousand! And none of the 00.1 percent variations is of significance in terms of the message the Bible conveys![3]

Christian concern for establishing the reliability of the biblical texts is based on commitment to the authority of God's written Word. Respect for the authority of this Word springs from the pages of the Bible itself. Speaking about Old Testament Scripture, Jesus the Messiah said, "For truly, I say to you, till heaven and earth pass away, not an iota, not a dot, will pass from the law until all is accomplished" (Matt. 5:18). Even the dots and the commas were considered significant by Jesus!

One of the most severe warnings in the Bible is against those who would attempt to change the inspired Word of God. In the Revelation in the last chapter of the Bible we read,

> I warn every one who hears the words of the prophecy of this book: If any one adds to them, God will add to him the plagues described in this book, and if any one takes away from the words of the book of this prophecy, God will take away his share in the tree of life and in the holy city, which are described in this book. (Rev. 22:18-19)

Although this warning is directed specifically against those who would tamper with the prophecies of the book of Revelation, many Christians sense that is it also a general warning to all those who tamper with any part of God's written Word. Christians, who believe that the Bible is God's inspired Word, seek to make certain that the texts handed on for scores of generations over many hundreds of years are accurate and reliable.

Christians believe the Bible should be translated into the languages of people. The biblical message is that God has chosen to reveal himself to humankind. God's revelation is understood best when communicated in one's native language. For this reason, as early as the third century after Christ, Christians were translating the Bible from Hebrew and Greek into local languages. The Syriac language in Syria was probably the first, then Egyptian, Latin in North Africa, and Ge'ez in Ethiopia. Today translating the Bible into local languages is one of the most important tasks of Christian missionaries. At least some portions of the Bible have already been translated from the original Hebrew and Greek texts into more than two thousand languages in countries around the world. The church desires to continue translating the Bible until all people everywhere can read God's written Word in their own native tongue.

Summary
Christians believe the Bible is God's written Word. The Bible is the witness and record of God's actions in the history of the covenant people and of his creation of a new covenant through Jesus the Messiah. The Bible contains the inspired prophetic interpretations of God's actions.

A MUSLIM RESPONSE
The Qur'an is very respectful of the Torah (Taurat), the Psalms (Zabur), and the Gospels (Injil), which form the major part of the Christian Scriptures. These Scriptures are acknowledged as true divine guidance. The prophets to whom these Scriptures were revealed (Moses, David, and Jesus) are believed to be great prophets of Allah and Islam. For a Muslim to deny the prophethood of Moses (Musa), David (Daud), or Jesus (Isa) is to deny the true teachings of Islam.

On the other hand, the Christian view of revelation and Scriptures is significantly different from the Muslim witness. The Christians believe the Bible has been inspired (breathed in by God) but not dictated by God, that the imprint of human personality is part of the content of biblical revelations, and that the Messiah (Jesus) himself is the *injil* (gospel).

However, according to Muslim witness, revelation which is contained in Scriptures or divine books is the true guidance sent down (tanzil) directly from God. It is God's Word revealed to chosen prophets. Gifted personalities as the prophets were, their lives and histories did not form part of the divine message or scriptural message. For the same reason the hadith, important as it is for Muslim belief, is not part of the Holy Qur'an.

It is unfortunate that the Christians do not acknowledge the final and perfect revelation of God—the Qur'an.

Notes

1. W. F. Albright, *From the Stone Age to Christianity* (New York: Doubleday, 1957), pp. 249-272.

2. *Gospel* is an English translation of the Greek word *euaggellion* which is commonly known as evangel. Euaggellion or evangel means the good news. The Arabic equivalent of the Evangel is *injil*. Consequently Muslims refer to the gospel as *injil*. In Swahili the word *injili* is used.

3. Sean Kealy, *The Changing Bible* (Nairobi: KUC, N.D.), p. 87.

For no prophecy ever came by the impulse of man, but men moved by the
Holy Spirit spoke from God (2 Peter 1:21).

18
The Prophets in History

THE CHRISTIAN UNDERSTANDING

The Bible tells the story of God's redemptive acts in history and contains the revealed interpretation of these redemptive acts. It is through the prophets and apostles that God interprets his redemptive acts in history.

We can illustrate biblical revelation by using one example: the birth of the Messiah as recorded and interpreted by the apostle Matthew (Matt. 1:18—2:23). Before Joseph and the virgin Mary were married, Mary was found to be with child through the Holy Spirit. An angel interpreted to Joseph and the virgin Mary the meaning of the virgin's miraculous conception. The promised Savior was born in Bethlehem.

Wise men from the east saw a special star and recognized that it was a sign from God that the Messiah (king) had been born. They went to Jerusalem in Judea with gifts, seeking the child. In Jerusalem they met with King Herod of Judea and scholars who knew the Old Testament prophecies concerning the Messiah. The wise men were told that the Messiah was to be born in the nearby town of Bethlehem. They went on to Bethlehem, where they found Jesus with Mary and Joseph. They praised God that the Savior had been born and gave him costly gifts—gold, frankincense, and myrrh.

An angel warned them not to return to Jerusalem, for King Herod wished to know where the baby was staying so he could kill him. Later, when Herod heard that the wise men had returned to their homes another way, he was furious and ordered the death of all the boy babies in Bethlehem two years old or younger. Nevertheless, Jesus was saved from death because an angel warned the family to flee into Egypt before Herod's troops arrived in Bethlehem. After Herod had died, Mary, Joseph, and the child Jesus returned to their homeland and lived in the town of Nazareth. All of this was a fulfillment of the Old Testament prophecies concerning the birth and childhood of Jesus the Messiah.

That is the story, briefly told. The story includes three revelation elements: event, response, interpretation. All three are inseparably merged; all three are revelation. *The event* in the account is God's redemptive act—the birth of the Messiah. *The response* is twofold: the wise men believe but King Herod does not believe. Herod fights against the child, against God's redemptive act, against God himself. The *interpretation* of the story makes it meaningful: the Savior has been born. Some people reject him; others accept him. To believe or not to believe, that is the issue. This is the nature of all biblical revelation: event, response, interpretation.

The Bible reveals that God invites us into a covenant relationship with himself. He acts redemptively in our own historical experience. The Bible records countless descriptions of God's redemptive acts. Here are a few examples.

> God saved Noah and his family from the flood.
> God saved the life of the son of the prophet Abraham through the sacrifice of a ram.
> God appeared to the prophet Moses in a burning bush.
> God delivered the people of the covenant from slavery under Pharaoh.
> God led the Israelites through the Red Sea on dry land.
> God fed them manna in the wilderness when there was no food.
> God gave them the Ten Commandments at Mount Sinai.
> God gave them water from the rock in the desert.
> God preserved their clothing and shoes.

The acts of God go on and on. He is involved redemptively in human experience. These acts of God are the central aspect of all divine revelation. God is known by what he does; that is the focus of the biblical view of revelation. Consequently a major part of the Bible is a description of what God has done in history, including the birth of Jesus the Messiah.

The acts of God, however, never take place in a historical vacuum. Whenever God acts, people respond in acceptance or rejection, in belief or nonbelief, in repentance or rebellion. The Bible reveals that God's redemptive acts call for human response. Consequently the Bible also describes the human response to God's redemptive acts. The Bible is a record of God's encounter with humanity and the human response to God.

The descriptions of the human response to God reveal the nature of the human heart. We see ourselves in the story of the wicked King Herod who hated anyone who threatened his position. We also see ourselves in the wise men who sought for the truth. The biblical description of the human response to God is an important aspect of revelation, because through it we recognize who we are and see our own need for redemption.

The act of God, the human response: these two dimensions of the God-human relationship are inseparable dimensions of biblical revelation. Only through divine revelation can we really understand the meaning of the divine-human encounter. This is the mission of the apostles and prophets of God. Through divine inspiration God revealed to the apostles and prophets the meaning of the acts of God and man's response to those acts.

We often read in the Bible that the prophet "saw" or "heard" the Word of the Lord (Isa. 1:1, Obad. 1:1, Mic. 1:1, Hab. 1:1). That was divine revelation. God revealed the true interpretation of his acts to the apostles and prophets. They proclaimed that interpretation through preaching, teaching, or writing. It is through the prophetic interpretation of God's saving acts in history that we recognize God's redemptive presence.

The apostle Matthew recorded the event; he described the human response; he interpreted what was happening: his name is Jesus, "for he will save his people from their sins" (Matt. 1:21). That is biblical revelation: history and interpretation. The act of God, the human response, the inspired interpretation—the three together are biblical revelation.

A MUSLIM RESPONSE

Muslims stress that the continued appearance of prophets at various times in history, among different peoples, shows the continuity of God's guidance and his active interest in man's well-being in this world and hereafter.

Christians emphasize divine inspiration as the way God revealed the true interpretation of his acts. Muslims, while not ruling out divine inspiration for prophets, are of the view that God sent down (*anzala, tanzil*) divine revelation to his messengers. Allah gave the message to the angel Jibril, who communicated it in direct speech. The prophets expressed that direct speech exactly as they heard it from the angel.

In the Qur'an, Allah uses the following terms for revelation: *anzala* (Qur'an 6:92), *uhiya* (Qur'an 6:94), *awha* (Qur'an 26:63), *nazzala* (Qur'an 25:1), *ata* (Qur'an 2:87), *tanzil* (Qur'an 36:5). All these terms suggest that he reveals the message or sends it down through an agent, not that he himself comes down (*nuzul*). All divine revelation expresses the absolute legal sovereignty of Allah. The inspired knowledge of saints and mystics is far below and incomparable to the revelation of God's will through his prophets.

Prophetic revelation in Islam transcends history. Neither historical events nor the human response to those events is in any sense revelation. Although the prophet stands in history, the revelation which he receives is not affected by his history. Revelation comes only from God. That is the Muslim witness.

A CHRISTIAN CLARIFICATION

When Christians refer to the inspiration of Holy Scriptures, they mean that these writings have been "breathed" by God through prophetic personhood. The concept is not equal to the more ordinary experience of inspired spirituality by mystics. The term *nuzul*, suggesting the coming down of divine personal presence, is a more appropriate interpretation of the Christian understanding of revelation than is *tanzil*, sent-down revelation. In a sense, all biblical revelation has an incarnational quality about it. Revelation as *nuzul* involves a profound experience of God-human relationship, a relationship which compromises neither the sovereignty of God nor the personhood of the man or woman.

You shall call his name Jesus, for he will save his people from their sins
(Matthew 1:21b).

19
Jesus the Messiah

THE CHRISTIAN WITNESS CONCERNING THE MESSIAH

The life and teaching of Jesus the Messiah is recorded in the four Gospels: Matthew, Mark, Luke, and John. These four books are accounts describing the life and teachings of the Messiah, who is the gospel (injil). Each of the Gospels were recorded by apostles or men who were associates of apostles. We believe they are authentic witnesses.

In this chapter we will give a biographical sketch of Jesus the Messiah, then make some interpretive comments.

The life and teachings of Jesus

As mentioned in the previous chapter, Jesus the Messiah was born in the town of Bethlehem in Judea in Palestine. The year was probably 4 B.C.; Caesar Augustus was ruler of the Roman Empire. The angel Gabriel told the virgin Mary that she would give birth to the Messiah: "The Holy Spirit will come on you, and the power of the Most High will overshadow you; therefore the child to be born will be called holy, the Son of God (Luke 1:35).

Just before Jesus' birth, Mary and Joseph traveled about 200 kilometers south from Nazareth in Galilee to Bethlehem in Judea for a Roman census. Because all lodging places were filled, they had to stay in a cattle stable. That is where Jesus was born. Angels announced his birth to shepherds on the nearby hills. These herdsmen came to see Jesus and found him with Mary and Joseph, just as the angels had said. Later wise men from the east also came to see Jesus. In the last chapter we described their visit, and the subsequent flight of Joseph, Mary, and Jesus into Egypt to escape Herod's anger.

After returning from Egypt, the family settled in Nazareth in Galilee. That is where Jesus grew up, probably as a carpenter, for that was the occupation of Joseph. We do not know much about his boyhood. One incident is recorded in Luke—when he was twelve Jesus went with Joseph and Mary to Jerusalem to worship the Lord. During that visit he astonished the religious leaders with his understanding of the Scriptures.

Jesus the Messiah began his public ministry when he was about thirty years old. The event which marked the beginning of his ministry was his baptism in the river Jordan by John the Baptist (John the Baptist is known as the Prophet Yahiya by Muslims). The gospel as recorded by Luke describes Jesus' baptism in this way:

> When Jesus also had been baptized and was praying, the heaven was opened, and the Holy Spirit descended on him in bodily form, as a dove, and a voice came from heaven, "Thou art my beloved Son; with thee I am well pleased." (Luke 3:21-22)

Immediately after his baptism, Jesus was led by the Spirit of God into the wilderness where he fasted for forty days. After that Satan tempted him severely. Satan tempted Jesus to turn stones to bread. He tempted Jesus to prove his power by jumping off a pinnacle of the temple. Satan tempted Jesus to bow down before him; Satan offered Jesus all the kingdoms of the world. These temptations are signs of the common human temptations to lust for wealth, power, and fame. Jesus quoted the Old Testament, showing that these temptations were against the revealed Word of God. Finally Satan left him, and the angels of God came to minister to him.

After the period of temptation, Jesus began his public ministry, which lasted about three years. He traveled in Judea and Galilee but also crossed national boundaries into regions such as Decapolis north of Galilee.

It is impossible to capture the breadth and meaning of Jesus the Messiah in a few paragraphs. He opened his ministry in his home town of Nazareth by startling the normal Sabbath congrega-

tional worship in the local synagogue with a reading from the
prophet Isaiah.

> The Spirit of the Lord is upon me,
>> because he has anointed me to preach good news to the
>> poor.
> He has sent me to proclaim release to the captives and recover-
>> ing of sight to the blind, to set at liberty those who are op-
>> pressed,
>> to proclaim the acceptable year of the Lord. (Luke 4:18-19)

After reading, he proclaimed, "Today this scripture has been fulfilled in your hearing" (Luke 4:21). In this manner Jesus announced
that in him the kingdom of God had broken into human history.
The new covenant was established. Jesus the Messiah demonstrated the breakthrough of God's kingdom throughout the rest of his
ministry.

Jesus was a miracle worker
Jesus healed the blind, lepers, lame, and deaf. He cast out multitudes of evil spirits. He raised the dead. On one occasion he fed five
thousand men, besides women and children, with only five loaves
of bread and two small fishes. Another time he fed four thousand
men, besides women and children, with seven loaves of bread and
several small fishes. In his hands the food multiplied. Once he
walked from land across the water to meet and comfort his disciples who were caught in a storm in the middle of the Sea of Galilee.
He calmed the storm. The people gave joyous witness that he was
"mighty in deed" (Luke 24:19).

Jesus as an outstanding teacher
Jesus used parables with great effectiveness. A parable is a story
from ordinary life which communicates truth. Many of his parables
communicated the meaning of the kingdom of God. Some are
short: "The kingdom of heaven is like leaven which a woman took
and hid in three measures of flour, till it was all leavened" (Matt.
13:33). Others are longer. The prodigal son left his father's house,
squandered his wealth and health in riotous living. When he came

to his senses, he returned to his father, who saw him when he was still a great way off and ran to meet him. The father embraced his son and ordered a great feast. The older son who had never left home was furious that his lost younger brother had been welcomed home with joy and feasting (Luke 15:11-32).

Jesus also taught through dialogue. He asked questions of people and led them into the truth as they sought the answers to the questions he asked. Jesus was a great preacher too. Audiences of several thousand would sit for many hours listening to his sermons, and "the crowds were astonished at his teaching, for he taught them as one who had authority, and not as their scribes" (Matt. 7:28-29).

Opposition to Jesus

Slowly opposition against Jesus developed. This happened for several reasons. First, Jesus was ruthlessly critical of all forms of false religion. He condemned religious hypocrisy and welcomed sinners to be his friends. He declared, "I have not come to call the righteous, but sinners to repentance" (Luke 5:32). This angered the religious leaders who had proud and superior attitudes.

Second, Jesus forgave sins. The religious leaders were furious because they said that only God could forgive sins. Nevertheless, Jesus affirmed that "the Son of man has authority on earth to forgive sins" (Matt. 9:6).

Third, Jesus said, "I and the Father are one" (John 10:30). When Jesus said that, the religious leaders accused him of blasphemy and tried to stone him. But Jesus pointed out that no one could do the works that he did unless God was in him. He said that the works he did proved that "the Father is in me, and I am in the Father" (John 10:38).

Fourth, Jesus proclaimed that the kingdom of God had come. At that time Palestine was under the colonial rule of Rome. The Jewish leaders thought the kingdom of God meant political independence from Rome. Many Galilean Jews tried to force Jesus to become king. They were disappointed because he refused to become the kind of king they wanted. He did not lead a military insurrection against Roman colonial rule. Consequently, in disappointment and frustration, many turned against him.

The crucifixion and resurrection

These crosscurrents of opposition increased during the last months of Jesus' ministry. Finally he headed south from Galilee where, as mentioned above, a popular movement had attempted to install him as the ruler of the Jews. As he traveled slowly south to Jerusalem in Judea, he warned his disciples that he would be crucified. At the Passover festival in Jerusalem, he was arrested and tried in both the Jewish and Roman courts. Although no two witnesses could agree on the charges, he was finally condemned to death. Mark records the trial in the Jewish court.

> Again the high priest asked him, "Are You the Christ, the Son of the Blessed?" And Jesus said, "I am; and you will see the Son of man sitting at the right hand of Power, and coming with the clouds of heaven." And the high priest tore his garments, and said, "Why do we still need witnesses? You have heard his blasphemy. What is your decision?" And they all condemned him as deserving death.   (Mark 14:61-64)

Although the Roman authorities in the Roman court saw no reason why he should be crucified, under mob pressure the government finally accepted a charge that he claimed to be King of the Jews. That was the charge nailed to the cross above his head when he was crucified.

Each gospel writer described the crucifixion. Jesus was beaten. He was mocked and slapped. Soldiers put a crown of thorns on his head and beat it into his skull. Finally he was nailed to the cross between two criminals. For three midday hours, darkness covered the land. "When Jesus had received the vinegar, he said, 'It is finished!' and he bowed his head and gave up his spirit" (John 19:30).

Friends of Jesus buried him in a new tomb carved in rock near the place of the crucifixion. The tomb was owned by a rich man Joseph of Arimathea. Jesus was in the grave until dawn on the third day. Then he arose from the dead. Several women and then some of his disciples discovered on Sunday morning that the grave was empty. After that Jesus appeared several times to his disciples. First he appeared to one of the women, Mary Magdalene; then to two of the disciples walking on the road to Emmaus; then to more disciples. He appeared at least eleven times during the next forty days. He ate with the disciples and conversed with them. They knew he was the risen Messiah. Finally he took them to a hill outside Jerusalem and was received into heaven.

In a later chapter, we will discuss the continuing presence of the glorified Messiah in the life and ministry of the church. Here we have limited our discussion to a brief review the earthly ministry of Jesus and the crucifixion and resurrection events. The life, death, and resurrection of Jesus the Messiah are astonishing and marvelous events. Many details of his life had been carefully and accurately foretold by the Old Testament prophets. Nevertheless, for many people Jesus seems unbelievable. The apostle John, however, writes that "these are written that you may believe that Jesus is the Christ, the Son of God, and that believing you may have life in his name" (John 20:31). Later the apostle says that he is "the disciple who is bearing witness to these things, and who has written these things; and . . . know[s] that his testimony is true" (John 21:24).

Who is Jesus the Messiah?

It is impossible to interpret Jesus the Messiah in a few short pages. Thousands of books have been written about him; hundreds of new books which attempt to interpret him are published every year. All are inadequate. These few pages are also insufficient. Yet Christians must attempt to give witness, although we confess that the witness we give cannot adequately convey the mystery and the depth of who Jesus is.

We will attempt to interpret Jesus briefly by introducing some of the names biblical writers have used to describe him. These names give different portraits of Jesus. Each is significant and true. Each is also inadequate. Yet the names can be helpful signs pointing us toward recognition of who Jesus is.

The Son of man

Jesus almost always referred to himself as the Son of man. This shows that he is an authentic human being. He is the true Son of Adam. He identifies with us totally. He was born into a poor family. He became a refugee when less than two years of age. He worked for a living as a carpenter. He experienced suffering and misunderstanding. He is a real man who understands us fully. He is Son of man.

The suffering servant

Several hundred years before the Messiah came, God had revealed to the prophet Isaiah that the coming Messiah would be a suffering servant. Isaiah wrote, "He was despised and rejected by men; a man of sorrows, and acquainted with grief; and as one from whom men hide their faces he was despised, and we esteemed him not" (Isa. 53:3). In the Messiah we see this prophecy fulfilled. He served humankind as a humble servant.

On one occasion the Messiah revealed a deep sign of his servant ministry by washing his disciples feet! In Palestine it was normal for the servant of the household to wash the feet of the master of the home when the master entered the house after a day's work or a journey. But Jesus took the place of the servant. He took a towel and washed and dried the feet of his beloved disciples! They were astonished, but he told them, "I have given you an example, that you also should do as I have done to you" (John 13:15).

All who recognize Jesus as the Messiah should also become servants to one another, just as Jesus became a servant to his disciples and to the people of his day. In fact, Jesus gave himself in servant ministry so completely that he suffered in doing good. He walked the paths of Palestine ministering to the needs of hundreds and thousands of people. His suffering servanthood climaxed in the crucifixion when he poured out his life for us. Jesus the Messiah was the perfect servant who gave his life in service for humankind. Through his suffering, redemptive servanthood, we are healed and made whole. As servant, he provides us with all we need.

The Lamb

When the Messiah came to John the Baptist to be baptized, John cried out, "Behold the Lamb of God who takes away the sin of the world!" (John 1:29). In most human societies, people offer animal sacrifices, hoping for the forgiveness of their sins. For example, the Bible describes a ram being sacrificed in place of a son of Abraham. Such sacrifices are signs that help us understand that humankind needs to be redeemed through a perfect sacrifice. Christians believe these offerings are a sign pointing to the Messiah who gave his life for our redemption from sin. He is the perfect Lamb of God. Through his sacrificial death and resurrection, we are forgiven and redeemed (Rev. 5:9).

The Son of God

This name was not invented by the disciples. Twice in Jesus' ministry he is addressed as "my Son" by a voice from heaven. First, at his baptism a voice from heaven said, "Thou art my beloved Son; with thee I am well pleased" (Luke 3:22). At the climax of Jesus' ministry, he and three of his disciples were on the Mount of Transfiguration alone. A cloud of glory covered them, the prophets Moses and Elijah miraculously appeared, then a voice from the cloud said, "This is my Son, my Chosen; listen to him" (Luke 9:35). These two events reveal that God himself addressed Jesus as "my Son."

Jesus accepted the name Son of God for himself. On one occasion, he asked his disciples who they believed he was. We read,

> Simon Peter replied, "You are the Christ, the Son of the living God." And Jesus answered him, "Blessed are you, Simon Bar-Jona! For flesh and blood has not revealed this to you, but my Father who is in heaven."   (Matt. 16:16-17)

The name Son of God reveals a perfect fellowship of love between Jesus and God the Father. We have already mentioned that humans are created in the image of God, that Adam and Eve were created as sons and daughters of God. Before they disobeyed, they knew and enjoyed complete spiritual fellowship with God. Throughout the Old Testament, people were invited into a covenant relationship with God. God was pleased to invite people to become his covenant children. The people of the covenant were invited to accept God as their heavenly Father. Jesus, as Son of God, is the one who experienced a perfect God-human relationship.

Jesus' experience of fellowship with God was perfect. He was the perfect image of God. He was the perfect human being. He was the one whose relationship with God was so clear and perfect and open and right that he was indeed the Son of God. So intimate was his relationship with the Father that Jesus could say with absolute humility and truthfulness, "I and the Father are one" (John 10:30).

Immanuel

The prophet Isaiah, writing many centuries before the birth of the Messiah, prophesied that his name would be "Immanuel" (Isa. 7:14). The apostle Matthew recalled this prophesy when he told of the virgin birth of Jesus. Matthew pointed out that Isaiah's prophesy affirmed that the one born of the virgin would be Immanuel, which in the Hebrew language means "God with us" (Matt. 1:23).

The witness of the New Testament is that God revealed himself fully in Jesus Christ. He is "God with us." The apostolic witness throughout the New Testament is that "God was in Christ." The apostle Paul wrote under the inspiration of God, "He [Christ] is the image of the invisible God, the first-born of all creation; . . . For in him all the fullness of God was pleased to dwell" (Col. 1:15, 19). Jesus himself said, "He who has seen me has seen the Father; how can you say, 'Show us the Father'?" (John 14:9). God made himself known to us in Jesus Christ. Because of Jesus, God is not a stranger.

The Word

Jesus is also called the Word of God. The gospel witness, according to the apostle John, begins,

> In the beginning was the Word, and the Word was with God, and the Word was God. He was in the beginning with God; all things were made through him, and without him was not anything made that was made. . . . And the Word became flesh and dwelt among us, full of grace and truth; we have beheld his glory, glory as of the only Son from the Father. (John 1:1-3, 14)

We know that God never sleeps. He is always expressing himself, and God's self-expression is creative. The self-expression of God is the Word, and when God speaks, creation happens. Through God's speech or word, the universe was created. In Jesus the Messiah, God's eternal self-expression, his everlasting Word, become flesh.

The Word of God is eternal, just as God is eternal. It is for this reason that the Messiah, as the incarnation of the eternal Word of God, could say that "before Abraham was, I am" (John 8:58). As the incarnation of the Word of God, the Messiah is eternal and uncreated. He is not begotten by God, because he is the eternal uncreated Word of God who "was in the beginning with God" (John 1:2a).

Jesus the Messiah is the living, eternal Word of God in human form. The Bible is God's written Word, but Jesus the Messiah is the incarnation of the eternal, personal, living Word of God. The apostle John wrote,

> That which was from the beginning, which we have heard, which we have seen with our eyes, which we have looked upon and touched with our hands, concerning the Word of Life . . . that which we have seen and heard we proclaim also to you.
>
> (1 John 1:1, 3).

The purpose of the Bible is to reveal to us the living Word, who is Jesus the Messiah. Jesus said, "You search the scriptures, because you think that in them you have eternal life; and it is they that bear witness to me" (John 5:39).

Many other names are also given to Jesus. They include Rabbi or Teacher, Prophet, King, Lord, Savior, Judge, and Redeemer. We could add to the list some of the "I am" statements of Jesus. I am the resurrection; I am the life; I am the truth; I am the way. We readily recognize that Jesus Christ cannot be fully captured by any name or cluster of titles. The Christian witness is that we are invited to meet Jesus the Messiah and respond to him with joy.

A MUSLIM RESPONSE

Muslims have great respect and love for Jesus (Isa) the Messiah. He is one of the greatest prophets of Allah. To deny the prophethood of Jesus is to deny Islam. Muslims sincerely believe that Jesus (PBUH) was born of a virgin mother, Maryam (Mary), by Allah's divine decree. He is referred to in the Qur'an as the son of Mary.

The Qur'an teaches that the coming of the Messiah was "glad tidings" (Qur'an 3:45). It describes his birth in this manner:

> Then we sent unto her [Mary], Our spirit and it assumed for her the likeness of Man. She said Lo! . . . He said I am only a messenger of thy Lord, that I may bestow on thee a faultless boy. She said: How can I have a boy when no mortal hath touched me. . . .

He said: (So it will be) Thy Lord saith. It is easy for me. And (it will be) that we may make of him a revelation for humankind and a mercy from us, and it is a thing ordained.   (Qur'an 19:7-21)

On the other hand, Muslims are genuinely opposed to the belief by Christians that Isa (PBUH) was divine or "Son of God." The basis of Muslim objection is Qur'anic. Allah says, "It is not befitting to (the Majesty of Allah) that He should beget a son. Glory be to him, when he determines a matter, He only says to it 'Be' and it is there" (Qur'an 5:75).[1]

The Qur'an testifies that Isa (PBUH) commanded the children of Israel, to whom he was a messenger, to worship "Allah, mine Lord and your Lord." So to the Muslims, Isa (PBUH) was human like the earlier prophets and not an incarnation of God. The Qur'an explicitly states, "No son did Allah beget nor is there any god along with Him."

This is the point where Muslims and Christians painfully part company. The issue is deeply theological and anthropological. The Christian view of incarnation seems to compromise God's transcendence and sovereignty while at the same time exalting a mere man to God-like status. By denying the incarnation, Islam is really affirming both the absolute transcendence of God and the rightful status of man as the servant and khalifa of God on earth.

The gulf between Christians and Muslims is further widened by the Christian silence on and nonrecognition of Muhammad (MBUH) as the Seal of Prophets, and the final guidance (the Qur'an) that was revealed to him by God. Yet recently Deedat has convincingly shown that the Bible says something about Muhammad (PBUH)—in Deuteronomy 18:18, which reads, "I will raise them a prophet from among their brethren, like unto thee, and I will put my words in his mouth, and he shall speak unto them all that I shall command him."[2]

A CHRISTIAN CLARIFICATION
Christians agree with Muslims that God did not "beget" a son. To conceive of God as begetting a son would be a gross evil for it would suggest polytheism and furthermore be a base anthropomorphism. Christians agree that God did not beget nor ever shall beget a son.

Jesus the Messiah, as Son of God, reveals something completely different. He reveals a perfect relationship between God and the Messiah. The sonship of Christ is a description of perfect love and fellowship between God and the Messiah.

Recall that Christians believe that the Messiah is the incarnation of the eternal Word of God. God does not beget his Word! His Word is eternal, co-existent with God, the perfect self-expression of God.

The two concepts of Word and sonship need to be kept together to understand the Christian witness that the Messiah is Immanuel, God with us.

Notes

1. See also Qur'an 19:88-93; 18:4-5; 2:116-117; 6:101-102.

2. Ahmad Deedat, *What the Bible Says About Muhammad* (Durban: Islamic Propagations Centre, 49 Madressa Arcade, N.D.), pp. 1-28. In this book the author shows that in all ways Muhammad (PBUH) was like Moses and Jesus was unlike Moses. Moses and his people, the Jews, are here addressed as a racial entity and as such their brethren would undoubtedly be the Arabs, all stemming from the same father, Abraham, but with different mothers, Hagar and Sarah. He also points out that Muhammad (PBUH) (unlike Jesus) was illiterate and the words (revelation) were actually put into his mouth as exactly foretold in the prophecy that "I will put my words in his mouth" (Deut. 18:18). Muhammad (PBUH) is brother to the Israelites because he was a descendant of Ismailil the son of Abraham.

And all flesh shall see the salvation of God (Luke 3:6).

20
Salvation

THE CHRISTIAN EXPERIENCE

Nicodemus was a respected leader of the Jews who secretly came to Jesus at night to learn about salvation.

Jesus told him, "Truly, truly, I say to you, unless one is born anew, he cannot see the kingdom of God."

Nicodemus replied, "How can a man be born when he is old: Can he enter a second time into his mother's womb and be born?"

Jesus said, "Truly, truly, I say to you, unless one is born of water and the Spirit, he cannot enter the kingdom of God. That which is born of the flesh is flesh, and that which is born of the Spirit is spirit."

Nicodemus asked, "How can this be?"

Jesus continued, "God so loved the world that he gave his only Son, that whoever believes in him should not perish but have eternal life. For God sent the Son into the world, not to condemn the world, but that the world might be saved through him. (Read the whole conversation in John 3:1-21.)

This conversation reveals to us that God our heavenly Father sent his Son into the world to save humankind. Those who receive his Son, the Messiah, experience a new birth. This salvation experience is a miracle of the Spirit of God. God as Father, Son, and Spirit are united in loving redemptive action. Our acceptance and experience of the Trinity love of God is salvation.

Is that hard to understand? Don't worry. Nicodemus was perplexed too. Let us look more carefully at the redemptive work of God as Father, Son, and Holy Spirit. We need to believe and receive God's saving redemptive action as Father, Son, and Holy Spirit to experience salvation.

God our heavenly Father created us in the image of God. This means we are most truly human when we live in joyous fellowship with God. Adam and Eve and all of us have turned away from our heavenly Father, but God has never left us. Throughout history he has repeatedly invited people to become his covenant children of faith, to repent, and to enter into the experience of redemption and salvation.

Nevertheless, our sinfulness always prevents us from experiencing perfect fellowship with God. We are unable to live righteously because we are sinful.

The prophet Isaiah lamented, "We have all become like one who is unclean, and all our righteous deeds are like a polluted garment" (Isa. 64:6). Our sinfulness separates us from God. Even the prophet Moses could not meet God face-to-face (Exod. 33:18-23). We are ashamed and fearful. We know we are guilty. We experience insincerity and hypocrisy. Humankind has frequently tried to cover guilt with animal sacrifices or offerings. Yet the sense of a broken and imperfect relationship with God is always present.

We know that our sin has separated us from God. Although God invites people into covenant, humankind fails to live in the covenant. Although God commands repentance, we seldom hear or obey his call

Consequently, to save and redeem us from sin, God entered history in *Jesus Christ*, his beloved Son. Three dimensions of Jesus's life and work must be considered if we are to understand salvation.

First, the life of Jesus the Messiah revealed the kingdom of God. In fact, he was the breakthrough of the kingdom of God into history. He was the new creation, the new Adam, the Adam from heaven, who is the kind of Adam we should be (1 Cor. 15:45-50). God commanded Adam to have dominion over the earth, but Adam and all humankind have failed to have perfect dominion over earth. Yet it is not so with Jesus. The Messiah, the new Adam from heaven, had absolute dominion over nature. He walked on water. He calmed the raging storm. He healed the sick. He multiplied food. Jesus did have dominion over the earth.

We also know we should live sinless lives, but we don't live righteously. We should establish justice, but instead we often neglect the rights of those who are weaker than we are. Yet Jesus was

righteous. He lived justice. He never sinned. Jesus was the kind of
Adam we should be. He was Lord of nature. He was the sinless one,
he is the just one. He was the kingdom of God in human history.
He was the recreation, the authentic breakthrough of the gracious
will of God for all humankind. Jesus related to everyone with perfect power, authority, justice, and love. He was the authentic
human. In him the kingdom of God was fulfilled. In him we perceive salvation (Heb. 2:6-9).

Second, the crucifixion and death of Jesus the Messiah revealed
the love of God and the inner mystery of the kingdom of God. Because God is love, he will never impose his will on humankind.
Rather than force us to obey him, God has chosen to accept all our
hostility and violence and hate himself. God in the Messiah accepted our rebellion with suffering, self-giving love.

The whole of humankind is represented at the crucifixion of
Jesus the Messiah. Included are the religious leaders and the politi-
cians; the mob and the common man; the educated, wealthy, and
professional; the poor and dispossessed; women and men; slaves
and free; Europe, Asia, Africa, the world. All are involved in the
tragic crucifixion of Jesus. As he hung on the cross, they wagged
their heads and mocked, but Jesus held no bitterness or revenge.
Instead he cried out, "Father forgive them" (Luke 23:34). In that cry
of forgiveness, we recognize the horror of our sin and also the love
and forgiveness of God. Why rebel against God if he forgives, even
when we are crucifying the Messiah, the anointed one, the altogether righteous one, the Son of God? The cross revealed the love
and forgiveness of God in the most profound way. In that forgiveness we find we are accepted by God.

At the moment Jesus yielded his life on the cross, the curtain in
the temple in Jerusalem was miraculously torn in two from top to
bottom (Luke 23:44-45). This curtain was the barrier in the temple
which separated the holy place from the holy of holies. Israelites
believed that the glory of God was present in the holy of holies.
Only the high priest was permitted into the presence of the glory of
God, and that only once a year. When Jesus was crucified, the curtain hiding the glory of God from human view was torn in two.
That tear in the curtain was a sign that all the barriers between God
and man were removed through the death of Jesus Christ. There-

fore, we are forgiven. We are accepted. We can address God with joy and confidence as "Father." The barrier our sinfulness had created between God and us was removed forever.

By giving his life on the cross, Jesus the Messiah gave himself as the perfect sacrifice for our sins (Heb. 8-10). We have mentioned that many peoples offer sacrifices of offerings in the hope that these will cover their sins and save them from evil. In the Old Testament, the people were commanded to offer a multitude of sacrifices. Even Abraham offered a ram in sacrifice, and in this way the life of his son was saved by God. These were signs pointing to the perfect sacrifice for sin: Jesus the Messiah. We know that we deserve punishment because we are sinful. Jesus bore the punishment for our sin. In Christ, God himself accepted the grief and shame and punishment of our sinfulness. We know that "the wages of sin is death" (Rom. 6:23). Jesus suffered death for us so we can experience life. We read,

> But he was wounded for our transgressions,
>   he was bruised for our iniquities;
> upon him was the chastisement that made us whole,
>   and with his stripes we are healed.   (Isa. 53:5)

Third we experience salvation through the resurrection of Jesus the Messiah. When we separate ourselves from God, we experience death. Satan is the prince of the powers of death. He and all the evil angels and spirits he leads are champions of death. Satan was pleased when Jesus was crucified. Death is his business. Nevertheless, God raised Jesus Christ from the dead. The resurrection of the Messiah was the defeat of death. The power of Satan was broken. Death will not win. Resurrection and life will triumph.

God wants us to experience the new life revealed in the resurrection of Jesus Christ. Just as the Messiah rose from the dead, so we who believe will also rise from death into life everlasting. Although our biological bodies may die, at the end of history we will all be raised with new and glorified bodies, just as Jesus was raised from the dead (1 Cor. 15).

Just as the resurrection of Jesus Christ represents the defeat of Satan and the evil spirits who are the champions of death, so we also experience victory over all the evil spiritual powers of death when we open our lives to the power of the risen Messiah. God put all powers under the authority of the risen glorified Messiah. We who believe in him experience release from fear and freedom from slavery to all evil spirits and powers (Eph. 1:15-23).

God appointed the risen Messiah to be intercessor between God and people. The Bible says, "So also Christ did not exalt himself to be made a high priest, but was appointed by [God]" (Heb. 5:5). God appointed the glorified, risen Messiah to be our intercessor because the Messiah lived among us and understands us perfectly. He experienced the same temptations and sorrows we do, yet he never sinned (Heb. 2:18). Because God appointed the Messiah to be the perfect mediator between God and humans, Christians pray to their heavenly Father in the name of Jesus the Messiah. Jesus himself promised, "My Father will give you whatever you ask in my name" (John 16:23b, NIV).

The Spirit of God is also involved in our experience of salvation. Jesus told Nicodemus that he must be born of the water and the Spirit. What is the work of the Spirit in bringing salvation?

It was the Spirit who revealed the Word of the Lord to the prophets in the Old Testament. That same Spirit reveals the truth of God to us today. All that we have said concerning God and the life and work of Jesus the Messiah is meaningless unless we are open to the voice and witness of the Spirit of God. Through the Holy Spirit, we are guided into all truth. Through the Spirit, the life of the risen, triumphant Messiah becomes part of our own experience. When we repent and believe, the Spirit recreates the true image of God in us.

God promised, through the prophet Jeremiah, that he would make a new covenant with humankind by creating a new heart in each believer. This is a new creation. The Spirit of God performs this miracle of grace and power in the believer. In the New Testament we read, "This is the covenant that I will make with them after those days, says the Lord: I will put my laws on their hearts, and write them on their minds . . . I will remember their sins and their misdeeds no more" (Heb. 10:16-17).

Jesus the Messiah called this new covenant and new creation the new birth. When we accept God's saving love as revealed in Je-

sus the Messiah, the Spirit of God begins to recreate us. We begin
to live in the kingdom of God. We begin to experience the new creation from heaven which Jesus represented so perfectly. We become more and more like Jesus. We become people free to love
with joy.

We experience salvation when we receive God's love and forgiveness, which was revealed in Jesus the Messiah and which is
present with us now through the Holy Spirit of God. In the life,
death, and resurrection of Jesus Christ, God's love was perfectly revealed. Through the Holy Spirit we experience his love personally.
God sent his Son into the world "that the world might be saved
through him" (John 3:17). God has sent the Holy Spirit, "the Spirit
of his Son into our hearts, crying 'Abba! Father' " (Gal. 4:7). The
one true God whom we experience as Father, Son, and Holy Spirit,
in perfect unity, perfect love, and perfect oneness, redeems and
saves us through his self-giving love.

In the Hebrew language, the name Jesus means "Yahweh
saves." The salvation we experience through believing in Jesus
Christ includes:

Right and joyous fellowship with God; reconciliation with God.
Reconciliation with our fellow human beings.
Forgiveness of sins.
A new creation or new birth of the true image of God in us.
Personal wholeness and blessing.
The experience of the love of God and the joyous privilege of ad-
dressing God as Father.
The defeat of death; eternal life, and the assurance of bodily res-
urrection from the dead.
Victory over sin and all the evil spirits and powers.
Participation in the kingdom of God, now and eternally.

We could say much more. In its simplest and most profound meaning, salvation is the experience of the love of God. We experience
salvation by believing in and committing ourselves totally to Jesus
the Messiah, the one through whom God revealed himself as the
Savior who loves us redemptively.

After Christ rose from the dead and was received into heaven, two Christian leaders, Paul and Silas, were put in jail for casting evil spirits out of a slave girl in Philippi in Macedonia, Greece. That night an earthquake struck. The doors of the jail flew open. The jailer was about to kill himself for he feared that the prisoners had fled, but Paul and Silas told him none of the prisoners had fled.

Then the jailer asked, "What must I do to be saved?"

Paul and Silas answered, "Believe on the Lord Jesus and you will be saved, you and your household" (Acts 16:30-31).

The Christian witness is that people who believe in Jesus the Messiah experience salvation and become part of the new covenant community called the church. In the next chapter, we will discuss the nature and work of the church. We will also comment on God's plan for the church and the role of the church in the kingdom of God.

A MUSLIM RESPONSE

From the Christian experience, salvation centers on the mission and crucifixion of Jesus Christ. This view is indeed in contrast to the Muslim experience.

According to Islam, Jesus Christ (Isa) (PBUH), son of Mary, was a great apostle of God. He was made to follow the footsteps of the prophets and to confirm the Law sent down before him. He was given the gospel (ijil) as the light and guidance for humankind. The Qur'an relates, "And we will make him a Messenger unto the children of Israel, saying: Lo I come unto you with a sign from your Lord. And I come confirming that which was before me of the Torah" (Qur'an 3:49-50).

The prophet Isa (PBUH), like many prophets before him, performed miracles. He cured the insane and the blind, healed the lepers, raised the dead. He did these miracles by Allah's will. They were meant to serve as proof of the truth of his mission. The important role bestowed on the prophet Isa (PBUH) did not make him "Son of God" or single him out as the only Savior for humankind. In fact the prophet Isa (PBUH) was only a servant and messenger of Allah. The Qur'an says, "Not one of the beings in the heavens and earth but must come to (Allah) most gracious as servant" (Qur'an 19:93).

The Christian witness that man is forgiven because of the crucifixion of Jesus is not in line with the Muslim belief. The end of the prophet Isa (PBUH) on earth is blanketed in mystery, and many Muslims prefer not to go beyond the explanation given in the Qur'an. On this issue the Qur'an tells us,

> That they said (in boast); We killed Christ Jesus, the son of Mary, the Messenger of God! But they killed him not, nor crucified him, but it was made to appear to them; and those who differ, therein are full of doubts, with no (certain) knowledge, but only conjecture to follow. For surety, they killed him not. Nay, Allah raised him unto Himself; and Allah is ever Mighty wise (Qur'an 4:157-158).

According to the true belief of Islam, it would seem most inappropriate for the Messiah to die through a shameful crucifixion. God, who is just, would not permit the righteous Messiah to suffer in that manner. Muslims believe that Allah saved the Messiah from the ignominy of crucifixion much as Allah also saved the Seal of the Prophets from ignominy following the Hijrah.

Furthermore, Islam does not identify with the Christian conviction that man needs to be redeemed. The Christian belief in the redemptive sacrificial death of Christ does not fit the Islamic view that man has always been fundamentally good, and that God loves and forgives those who obey his will.

Islam is the way of peace. The Muslim view, which is in total contrast to the Christian experience, is that man experiences peace through total submission to God's guidance and mercy. Jesus Christ (PBUH), like many prophets before him, and Muhammad (PBUH) the Seal of Prophets, were both examples of God's mercy to humanity.

A CHRISTIAN CLARIFICATION

It may be that the Christian and the Muslim view of the crucifixion of Christ are closer together than appears on the surface. The gospel emphasizes that Jesus the Messiah gave his life. He said,

> I lay down my life, that I may take it again. No one takes it from me, but I lay it down of my own accord. I have power to lay it

down, and I have power to take it again; this charge I have received from my Father." (John 10:17-18)

The crucifixion of Christ was a drama of supreme self-giving. The Messiah himself gave his life; no one could take it from him, for certainly no one could slay the eternal Word of God. Although he gave himself unto death on the cross at the hands of evil people, they could not destroy him. He arose from the grave. Certainly Christians would agree that death did not triumph over the Messiah. In his resurrection, he triumphed over death.

The household of God . . . is the church of the living God, the pillar and bulwark of the truth (1 Timothy 3:15b).

21
The Church

THE CHRISTIAN COMMUNITY

The church was created by God at the feast of Pentecost fifty days after the death and resurrection of Jesus the Messiah. During his last post-resurrection appearance, Jesus told his disciples to wait in Jerusalem until they had received the Holy Spirit (Acts 1:4-5). Forty days after his resurrection, Jesus the Messiah was received into heaven. The disciples obeyed Jesus and remained in an upper room in Jerusalem, waiting for the Holy Spirit. They spent the time praying, fasting, and waiting. About 120 people were present (Acts 1).

The disciples waited for ten days until the Pentecost festival. This feast was a Jewish celebration of thanksgiving for the first fruits of the harvest. It was on Pentecost day that God blessed the disciples with the Holy Spirit. We read,

> And suddenly a sound came from heaven like the rush of a mighty wind, and it filled all the house where they were sitting. And there appeared to them tongues as of fire, distributed and resting on each one of them. And they were all filled with the Holy Spirit and began to speak in other tongues, as the Spirit gave them utterance. (Acts 2:2-4)

The sound of the event was heard outside, and people from different parts of Jerusalem came to hear and see what was happening. Each person heard the gospel proclaimed in his or her native tongue. "Parthians and Medes and Elamites and residents of Mesopotamia, Judea and Cappadocia, Pontus and Asia Phrygia and

Pamphylia, Egypt and the parts of Libya belonging to Cyrene, and visitors from Rome, both Jews and proselytes, Cretans and Arabians" (Acts 2:9-11). They were amazed because miraculously, as the disciples praised the Lord, each person heard the gospel (injil) in her or his native tongue.

The apostle Peter stood and began to preach the gospel to the assembled people. After they heard the gospel, they cried out, "Brethren, what shall we do?"

Peter answered, "Repent, and be baptized every one of you in the name of Jesus Christ for the forgiveness of your sins; and you shall receive the gift of the Holy Spirit" (Acts 2:37-38).

The people responded to the gospel and about three thousand were baptized that day. That was the beginning of the Christian church, which has now grown to include hundreds of millions of people living in almost every country on earth. What is this new community of faith created by God at Pentecost nearly two thousand years ago? What is the nature of the church which attracts millions of new believers into its fellowship every year? Who is the church?

Believing people are the church

We have already mentioned that during his ministry Jesus called twelve disciples to follow him. They came from different backgrounds. Several were fishermen by trade, another was a tax collector, and at least one had been a guerrilla freedom fighter (Luke 6:13-14). Jesus formed the disciples into a new community who recognized Jesus Christ as Lord.

The faith of the disciples was revealed in the response of Peter to Jesus' question, "Who do you say that I am?"

Peter answered, "You are the Christ, the Son of the living God."

Jesus responded, "On this rock, I will build my church, and the powers of death shall not prevail against it" (Matt. 16:16-18).

The church is the people who have believed in Jesus Christ and have received him as Lord and Savior. That is the rock on which the church is built.

Although Peter and the disciples did believe in Jesus the Messiah, they were weak in their faith. When Jesus was crucified, most of the disciples fled. Even Peter denied that he knew Jesus. Only after the resurrection of Jesus the Messiah and the mighty pouring out of the Spirit of God on the disciples on the day of Pentecost did they became bold witnesses to the gospel. When they were filled with the Spirit of God, they had power to witness and become the kind of people Jesus had intended when he said the powers of death could not stand against the church.

The church is the people who believe in Jesus Christ. The church is not a building, although we sometimes do refer to the place where Christians worship as a church. However, in the New Testament, the word *church* never refers to a building. In fact, for many generations, the early Christians did not meet in special buildings for worship. They met in homes. In many places even today, Christians worship in the homes of believers or under a shade tree! The people who believe in Jesus are the Christian church. Christian believers should meet regularly in the name of Jesus Christ. Christians in fellowship are the church.

Jesus said, "For where two or three are gathered in my name, there am I in the midst of them" (Matt. 18:20). Jesus, the glorified Messiah, is present in the midst of believers through the presence of the Holy Spirit. Whenever believers meet in the name of Jesus Christ, they sense that he is present among them. They pray in Jesus' name. Their prayers are answered. They confess their sins and experience in their spirits that they are truly forgiven. They ask for guidance and sense the guiding wisdom of the Lord. They ask for strength and find renewal, refreshment, power, peace, grace, and love. They know Jesus is indeed present in their midst as they meet in his name.

After meeting, Christians scatter to continue their normal work—teaching, farming, business, or whatever it is. Then again, perhaps a day later or a week later, they gather in the name of Jesus. Again they sense that he is present in their midst. They are the church—those who meet in the name of Jesus then scatter into the world. The church is the people who gather in Jesus' name and then scatter. The gathering and scattering community of Christian faith is the church.

Leadership in the church

The church has leaders and organization. The leadership plan for the church had its beginnings with Jesus and his disciples. After the death and resurrection of the Messiah, his closest associates were called by God to become apostles and leaders of the church. Soon the apostles needed administrative help to handle financial matters, especially in relation to the poor widows in the Jerusalem church. Under the guidance of the Holy Spirit, seven men were selected as apostolic assistants. They were ordained to their office by the apostles laying hands on them and praying for them (Acts 6:1-6). Later these apostolic assistants were called deacons.

As congregations of Christians began to multiply, each local congregation also needed leaders. These local leaders were selected under the guidance of the Holy Spirit after prayer and fasting. They were called elders and were also ordained by the laying on of hands by the apostles (Acts 14:23).

As the apostles grew older, and as the church became too large for them to give it sufficient leadership, bishops were chosen and ordained. As the apostles left the scene, bishops replaced them as the overall leaders of the church (2 Tim. 1:6-7). Thus we see that from the beginning, the church developed a three-office ministry: bishops, deacons to assist the bishops, and elders for the leadership of local congregations. All were ordained by the laying on of hands by the leaders of the church.

Today most Christian churches have a form of leadership somewhat similar to that which the early apostolic church developed. Of course, there are many variations, but the general pattern of ordained leadership is practiced in most churches. This simple but effective organization aids the church greatly in doing its work in the world.

Culture and the church

As the church grew, it began to experience considerable cultural differences in its fellowship. For example, the Jewish Christians practiced circumcision but Gentiles did not. Gentiles and Jews dressed differently and ate different food. The church was perplexed. Should all Christians have the same cultural practices? In the Old Testament, all the people of the covenant belonged to the same culture. Was this necessary in the new covenant? Circumcision was particularly difficult because in the Old Testament circumcision was the sign that a man was a member of the covenant community.

That issue finally led to a great conference, which was held in Jerusalem about A.D. 43. The apostles and other church leaders studied what the Old Testament said about the creation of the church through the power of the Spirit. They also listened to reports of what the Holy Spirit was doing in the lives of Gentile Christians who had become righteous people after receiving the gift of the Spirit of God. Finally the church decided that the Gentile Christians should be free to remain in their culture after becoming Christians. They did not have to follow Jewish or Old Testament dietary regulations or practices such as circumcision. However, they were to refrain from evil, such as sexual immorality and certain practices associated with idol worship (Acts 15:1-35).

This decision of the Jerusalem Conference is significant, for it determined forever that the Christian church should have cultural diversity. Wherever the gospel goes, people are invited to accept the good news of salvation through Christ, then to put the gospel into practice in their own local situation. They are to clothe their Christian experience in their own cultural clothing. It is for this reason that the Christian church has more cultural diversity than any other religious community on earth. Christians in every society are free to remain in their culture as believers in Jesus Christ.

Nevertheless, Christians also experience an amazing unity The Bible says, "There is one body and one Spirit, just as you were called to the one hope that belongs to your call, one Lord, one faith, one baptism, one God and Father of us all, who is above all and through all and in all" (Eph. 4:4-6). The unity of the church makes it possible for Christians to experience peoplehood and oneness even though culturally diverse. The Scriptures say, "There is neither Jew nor Greek, there is neither slave nor free, there is neither male nor female; for you are all one in Christ Jesus" (Gal. 3:28).

Diversity and cooperation in the church

Sometimes diversity has led to misunderstandings between Christians. Differences have led to the formation of particular Christian groups in the worldwide church. This is one cause for the formation of Christian denominations. For example, one reason for the development of the Anglican Church in England during the sixteenth century was the desire of the English people to have a national church which would affirm desirable aspects of English culture. This church was formed more for cultural and national reasons than for doctrinal or theological reasons. In a similar manner, some modern independent African churches have formed because of a desire to make Christianity more African. Many times denominations have developed because of the good and biblical desire to permit the gospel to flourish and grow in a particular culture.

Nevertheless, it is not always that way. Sometimes Christians have divided because of serious differences of opinion about what Christians should believe or practice. One such division is the separation between the Catholic Church and the Protestant churches. We do not have space for an in-depth discussion of the reasons for that sixteenth-century division. Yet we should mention that a main issue was different attitudes toward the Bible. Protestants believed the Bible should be the only basis of authority in the church. Catholics felt that the witness of the Holy Spirit through the church's traditions and leadership was also important. These different viewpoints concerning the basis of authority in the church helped contribute to the division between the Catholic and Protestant churches about 450 years ago. The Protestant church has also divided into denominations because of cultural or theological diversity.

Christians are aware that cultural diversity is right. Healthy Christian experience and commitment encourages variety. At the same time, Christians are painfully aware that divisions in the church which prevent good fellowship among Christians are sinful. They know such divisions are evidence that Christians do not have sufficient love for one another. They confess the sin of division. In our modern day, Christians are finding that sometimes the Holy Spirit is helping to unite divided Christians in fellowship as brothers and sisters in Jesus Christ. They are finding that the love of God helps them to overcome many of their differences. They are able to work together in a spirit of Christian love and cooperation, even though they might disagree on some things.

In some countries, councils of churches have been formed to

help Christians express love for and cooperation with one another. There are also world Christian fellowships, such as the World Council of Churches or the World Evangelical Fellowship, which help Christians work together in better ways. All over the world today, Christians are recognizing the sin of their divisions. They are trying to hear the voice of the Holy Spirit as they attempt to express love toward one another.

Millions of Christians desire to experience more fully the love which Christ prayed for just before his crucifixion when he asked "that they may become perfectly one" (John 17:23). We are not yet perfectly one! Yet the Spirit of God is working among Christians in many parts of the world today. He is helping them to accept both variety and unity in Christ.

A MUSLIM RESPONSE

The Umma, like the church, is not a building. It is a community of believers. While the church is people who have believed in Jesus Christ, received him as Lord and Savior, the Umma is that community which entirely submits to Allah and takes instruction from his Seal of Prophets (PBUH). Leadership in the church is not comparable to that of the Umma. The Umma has no ordained leaders after the fashion of the church. In the Umma, it is God's Word (Qur'an), the Sunnah (practice) of Prophet Muhammad (PBUH), and the Shari'a (God's divine Laws) that are the guiding principles of the Umma.

While appreciating that the church has accepted cultural diversity, we learn that at times this has led to misunderstanding among Christians, even causing divisions in the church. In contrast, Islam has come up with a single universal Islamic culture, generally common to the entire Umma. There is some diversity in the Umma, but ideally the Umma surpasses ethnic, national, linguistic, and racial boundaries. For this reason Muslims cannot talk of African, Turkish, Chinese, or American Islam. Perhaps for similar reasons the Umma has not experienced as many divisions as characterize the church today.

God is spirit, and those who worship him must worship in spirit and truth
(John 4:24).

22
Worship and Fellowship

THE CHRISTIAN PRACTICE

If you live near Christians, you will notice that at least once a week they gather in a home, under a tree, in a hall, or in a church building for worship. The place where Christians worship is not important. The significant aspect of Christian worship is the gathering of believers who worship the one true God who has revealed himself as Father, Son, and Holy Spirit. All true Christian worship recognizes God as Father, Savior, and Spirit who is present with us now. Christians recognize the triune nature of God in worship.

This is evident when Christians pray. They pray to God the loving heavenly Father, in the name of Jesus the beloved Son who has revealed God's redemptive love to humankind, and in the power of the Holy Spirit who is the presence of God in the lives of the believers. It is this Christian experience of the triune nature of God which is common to all Christian worship everywhere.

Otherwise there is no real commonality in Christian worship. Remember that at the Jerusalem Conference in A.D. 43, the church approved of cultural diversity. Ever since Christian worship has reflected considerable differences. Some Christians pray with loud voices with everyone praying at the same time. Others have only the leader of the congregation leading in the prayers. Some stand when they pray; others kneel. Some have a cross or lit candles at the front of the church, but others feel that these signs are not helpful and have no such symbols. For some Christians rituals are very important, but for others the preaching of the Word of God is the most significant aspect of worship. Christian worship practices have great diversity, but all are united in grateful celebration of the love of God our Father revealed to us through Jesus Christ and present with us now through the Holy Spirit.

Although Christians have great diversity in worship, several practices are common. We will mention a few.

Baptism
Before Jesus was received into heaven, he commanded his disciples to go into all the world and "make disciples of all nations, baptizing them in the name of the Father and of the Son and of the Holy Spirit, teaching them to observe all that I have commanded you" (Matt. 28:19-20). The disciples began to obey this command on the day of Pentecost, when they proclaimed the gospel and about three thousand people entered the church through believing in Jesus the Messiah and receiving baptism (Acts 2:37-42). The decision to believe and the act of baptism seemed to go together. Ever since that Pentecost day, the church has baptized believers who are accepted as church members.

Baptism is a ceremony involving (1) confessing one's faith in Christ before God in the presence of witnesses and (2) receiving baptism with water in the name of the Father, the Son, and the Holy Spirit. In some churches, infants are baptized, in which case the parents or guardians symbolically make the confession of faith on behalf of the child. Those who baptize infants consider it a sign that innocent children are also members of the covenant community. In all churches, water is used as a sign of cleansing, the fullness of the Spirit, and acceptance into the church. In some churches, only a few drops of water are sprinkled on the head. In other Christian communities, handfuls of water are used. In still others, the candidate for membership is dipped under the water as a sign that his or her sins are buried; the candidate rising out of the water after the baptism is a sign of rising with Christ to new and eternal life.

Some Christian groups baptize a person almost immediately after confession of faith in Jesus Christ, but most churches have a period of instruction before the new believer can be accepted for baptism. A new believer needs instruction for two reasons: (1) to teach the new believer the doctrines and practices of the church; (2) to have a period of time to see whether the new believer has experienced a change in conduct. Christians are to live righteously, and most churches require a period of time to know whether the new candidate for baptism has really experienced a change in life and conduct. After the completion of Christian instruction, a public baptismal service is held.

In churches which baptize infants, the practice is somewhat different. In these churches the young person baptized as an infant is invited to participate in confirmation classes when about twelve years old. These classes are similar to the catechetical classes a new believer has before baptism. After the church leaders are satisfied that the candidate for confirmation is a committed Christian and understands the doctrines and practices of the church, a confirmation service is held in which those baptized as infants are welcomed into the church as full members and invited to communion services.

Sunday worship

Christians should meet for worship and fellowship regularly. Some Christians meet daily. Many meet at least once a week. Normally the weekly meeting of Christians takes place on Sunday morning. This is because Jesus the Messiah rose from the dead on Sunday morning. The meeting of Christians on Sunday is a celebration and remembrance of the resurrection of Jesus.

The church service on Sunday mornings varies greatly from group to group. But in all Christian communities the central aspects of worship are confession and celebration in thanksgiving for salvation through Jesus Christ whom God sent into the world. In most churches reading the Bible is an important aspect of the worship service. Hymns are sung and prayers offered. Usually a leader proclaims the gospel in a sermon. Many churches also celebrate the eucharist or communion in the Sunday morning worship service.

The eucharist

The eucharist (communion or mass) is a remembrance of the death and resurrection of Jesus Christ. The Old Testament Passover festival helps us understand the meaning of the eucharist (Exod. 12). When God delivered the Hebrew peoples from slavery under Pharaoh, he commanded each family to sacrifice a perfect lamb only one year old and put blood of the sacrificed lamb on the two doorposts and lintel of the entrance to the home. Then the family met inside the home and ate the roasted flesh of the sacrificed lamb to give them strength for their journey.

While the Hebrew families were in their homes eating the roasted lamb, the angel of God passed through the land of Pharaoh and killed the oldest child in every house which did not have blood over the entrance. When the people of the land saw what had happened, they begged the Hebrews to leave. In Hebrew history this great event is called the Passover, because the angel of death passed over every house which had blood over the door.

In thanksgiving for what God had done for them, every year at Passover the Hebrew people remembered in a special way that God saved them from slavery and death. They recognized that the perfect lamb which they sacrificed was a sign of salvation.

Jesus was crucified at Passover time. On the night of his crucifixion, he ate the Passover meal with his disciples. During that supper, he took bread and broke it saying, "Take, eat; this is my body." Then he took a cup of wine and in a similar manner gave it to them saying,

> Drink of it, all of you; for this is my blood of the covenant, which is poured out for many for the forgiveness of sins. I tell you I shall not drink again of the fruit of the vine until that day when I drink it new with you in my Father's kingdom.   (Matt. 26:26-29)

This was the first eucharist or communion service. It was introduced by Jesus the Messiah himself.

The Christian church celebrates the eucharist rather than the Passover because Jesus introduced the eucharist at the Passover feast. In fact, Christians believe that the Old Testament Passover feast was a sign preparing people to understand and accept the crucifixion of Jesus as the perfect sacrifice for sin. The Passover was a sign pointing to the future sacrifice of Jesus on the cross.

The bread is a sign of the body of Christ. The wine is a sign of his blood given for our salvation and forgiveness when he offered himself for our redemption on the cross.

The eucharist is also a sign of unity. Jesus shared one cup and broke one piece of bread with his disciples. In the eucharist, the whole congregation drinks and eats together from one cup and one common piece of bread. In this way the church experiences a renewal of unity in the Christian fellowship. The eucharist is a profound celebration of unity in Christ.

The eucharist also reveals reconciliation between God and humans. The material emblems of the eucharist are signs of the redemptive presence of God among people. The material and the spiritual dimensions of life are united in the eucharist. The eucharist is a sign that the human, the creature, is invited to receive divine grace. It is a sign of eating, of fellowship, and of communion with God, our loving heavenly Father.

Service

Service is also a dimension of Christian worship. The marvelous gift of salvation, the recreating grace of God, the experience of the redemptive love of God, the presence of the Holy Spirit in the life of the believer—all of these release the disciple of the Messiah to serve freely and joyously. The Bible says, "I appeal to you therefore, brethren, by the mercies of God, to present your bodies as a living sacrifice, holy and acceptable to God, which is your spiritual worship " (Rom. 12:1).

True worship includes offering ourselves in sacrificial service to our fellow human beings. As a sign of self-giving service, most Christian congregations include the collection of money to be used in service to others as part of their worship expression. The giving of money in the worship experience is a sign that because God has redeemed us we also offer ourselves for others.

We have mentioned several significant aspects of Christian worship. All are important. Some Christians appreciate one aspect more than other aspects. For example, many Protestants consider preaching the central event in Christian worship. Others believe the central worship event is the fellowship with other believers. Catholics, especially, believe that the eucharist or mass is the central event. Still other groups may consider singing and rejoicing to be central, while others give prominence to praying for the sick and casting out evil spirits in the name of the risen glorified Messiah. These differences in emphasis do affect the way the worship services are conducted. For example, Protestant churches tend to have good sermons, while Catholic churches excel in communion ritual.

Yet the differences in worship practices should not obscure the one central event in all Christian fellowship. The meeting of Christians for worship is an expression and celebration of the unity and love of God. Christian worship is a participation, with thankfulness, in God's saving redemptive love. For this reason whenever Christians meet for worship, they sense that the promise of Jesus is true indeed: "Where two or three [or more] are gathered in my name, there am I in the midst of them" (Matt. 18:20). Through the presence of the Spirit of God in the worshiping congregation, Christians experience Jesus the Christ in their midst.

A MUSLIM RESPONSE

The Christian practice of worship is quite different from the Muslim practice. It is the Christian experience of the triune nature of God in worship which is common to all Christian worship everywhere. Otherwise there is no real commonality in Christian worship. The person of Jesus Christ is central in Christian worship.

For Muslims, worship is a wide term applied beyond prayer (salat). Worship (ibadah) is the submission that Allah is your master and you are his servant, and so all that the servant does in obedience to him is ibadah. Every good deed performed to seek the pleasure of Allah is worship. This can be an individual or a collective act. There are some rituals of ibadah which have been made compulsory, and if left out, one commits a sin or ceases to be a Muslim.

The most important duty of ibadah, after acknowledging the oneness of Allah, is the salat. The Muslim prayer, whether congregational or individual, unlike the Christian form of worship, is uniform all over the world. The ranks of the faithful, their unison in movement behind the imam (leader of prayer), facing the direction of the Qibla, the *raka'h* (unit) and the *sujud* (prostration), which brings the believer down to the earth—all these prayer rituals are performed in the same way. There is commonality in the language of the prayer and in almost every detail.

Prayer, the center of worship in Islam, is to none other than the almighty Allah. Prayer is to be offered directly to Allah, not through any intercessor.

For the kingdom of God does not mean food and drink but righteousness and peace and joy in the Holy Spirit (Romans 14:17).

23
Right Conduct

THE CHRISTIAN IDEAL

The Christian church does not have any organized system of universal law for right conduct. Sometimes in Christian history some groups have tried to make a systematic law for conduct, but this has never been acceptable to the church as a whole. Christians do not rely on a system of law to regulate their conduct because:

1. Jesus the Messiah taught, "You shall love the Lord your God with all your heart, and with all your soul, and with all your mind. This is the great and first commandment. And a second is like it, You shall love your neighbor as yourself. On these two commandments depend all the law and the prophets" (Matt. 22:37-40). Love is the key to all Christian morality. True love for one's neighbor can only come from the heart. It cannot be reduced to a set of rules. It is the inner attitude which is significant. Love for our fellow human beings is the basis of Christian conduct.

2. The Holy Spirit is present in us to guide us in the way of righteousness. Before Jesus was crucified, he promised that after he was received into heaven, God would send the Holy Spirit, who "will guide you into all the truth" (John 16:13). Jesus also promised that the Holy Spirit would "convince the world concerning sin and righteousness and judgment" (John 16:8). The Holy Spirit is the personal presence of God in the experience of the Christian believer and the church. The Holy Spirit guides the believer and the church in truth

and righteousness. It is impossible to reduce this kind of personal encounter with God who is the altogether righteous One into a formal ethical code. Christian righteousness springs from a fellowship relationship with God. It cannot be codified. It is too personal for that.

3. The Holy Spirit in the life of the Christian recreates the image of God that was spoiled when humans turned from God. God is interested in the recreation in righteousness of the person. Slavish obedience to laws does not recreate persons. They can think evil thoughts even though outwardly they might look righteous. Jesus was supremely concerned about the inner person where righteousness or evil originate. That is why Jesus berated the hypocritical religious leaders of his day, saying,

Woe to you, scribes and Pharisees, hypocrites! for you cleanse the outside of the cup and of the plate, but inside they are full of extortion and rapacity. You blind Pharisee! first cleanse the inside of the cup and of the plate, that the outside also may be clean. (Matt. 23:25-26)

Throughout the New Testament there is tremendous emphasis on the need to be transformed, to be re-created, to become like Christ in the inner person. The apostle Paul has written under the inspiration of the Holy Spirit,

Put off your old nature which belongs to your former manner of life and is corrupt through deceitful lusts, and be renewed in the spirit of your minds, and put on the new nature, created after the likeness of God in true righteousness and holiness.
(Eph. 4:22-24)

Recreated persons living under the guidance of the Holy Spirit need principles to help them measure whether they are indeed living in "the likeness of God in true righteousness and holiness." What principles of righteousness did the Holy Spirit reveal through the prophets in the past? What principles of righteousness did Jesus the Messiah teach? What characteristics of the truth does the Holy Spirit reveal to the people of the covenant today? We will look briefly at some basic moral teachings that have been revealed to us through both the prophet Moses and the life and teachings of Jesus the Messiah.

Much of the Torah consists of teachings on right conduct and worship, which God revealed to the prophet Moses. These principles for right conduct are summarized in the Ten Commandments God revealed to the people of the covenant at Mount Sinai (Exod. 20:1-17). A summary of these commandments is as follows:

1. You shall have no other gods except the one true God.
2. You shall not make for yourself an image to worship.
3. You shall not use the name of the Lord your God in a careless manner.
4. Remember the seventh day of the week, and keep it holy.
5. Honor your father and your mother.
6. You shall not kill.
7. You shall not commit adultery.
8. You shall not steal.
9. You shall not tell a lie about your neighbor.
10. You shall not covet anything that belongs to your neighbor.

Christians everywhere recognize that these Ten Commandments are right. All Christians should abide by principles revealed in the Ten Commandments. They are based on the principle of love of God and persons.

Elsewhere in the Torah, God revealed that we should love God and our neighbors (Deut. 6:4, Lev. 19:18). When Jesus the Messiah appeared, he pointed out that the commandment to love is the greatest commandment of all; all the other commandments in the Bible are summarized in the law of love. Jesus said that on these commandments to love "depend all the law and the prophets" (Matt. 22:40). It is for this reason that Jesus commanded his disciples to "love one another" (John 15:12). Through his life and teachings, Jesus the Messiah taught people the meaning of love.

In the previous chapter, we said that Jesus served people by healing them and caring for their needs. He welcomed and forgave sinners. The forgiveness he expressed through his crucifixion is the supreme revelation of love. However, it is not only his deeds which reveal love. His teachings are also helpful.

On one occasion Jesus took his disciples onto a mountain near the Sea of Galilee to teach them moral principles based on love. He explained to them that true righteousness depends on an inner spiritual commitment to God. These teachings are called the Sermon on the Mount and are recorded in Matthew, chapters 5—7.

Jesus the Messiah began the Sermon on the Mount by saying, "Blessed are the poor in spirit, for theirs is the kingdom of heaven" (Matt. 5:3). Christians believe that the kingdom is "righteousness and peace and joy in the Holy Spirit" (Rom. 14:17). Jesus said that the "poor" in spirit enter or inherit this kingdom. Only those who recognize that they are sinful, who recognize that they are not living in right fellowship with God, seek forgiveness. Only these "poor" people experience God's saving grace. The poor in spirit are willing to receive salvation through Jesus the Messiah. These are the needy people who open their lives to the recreating power of the Holy Spirit. They are the ones who enter the kingdom of heaven.

These "poor in spirit" people experience an inner renovation of attitudes which affects all their relationships. Jesus gave specific examples of the change of attitude which people who have entered the kingdom of heaven should experience. Here are several examples.

Peace (Matt. 5:21-26).
In the Ten Commandments we read, "You shall not kill." But Jesus the Messiah taught that hate is also wrong. It is hate which drives people to kill. We need to become free of evil attitudes toward other people. Jesus said, "I say to you that everyone who is angry with his brother shall be [in danger of] judgment" (Matt. 5:22).

Marriage (Matt. 5:27-32).
One of the Ten Commandments says, "You shall not commit adultery" (Exod. 20:14). But Jesus the Messiah said that any desire for a woman who is not one's wife is sin. He said, "I say to you that every one who looks at a woman lustfully has already committed

adultery with her in his heart" (Matt. 5:28). Adultery destroys the marriage and the adulterer. Adultery is evil. For this reason Jesus said that if any part of your body such as the eye tempts you into sin, it is better to have the eye plucked out than to yield to the temptation. "It is better that you lose one of your members than that your whole body be thrown into hell" (Matt. 5:29).

Jesus also taught that divorce is wrong. "I say to you that every one who divorces his wife, except on the ground of unchastity, makes her an adulteress and whoever marries a divorced woman commits adultery" (Matt. 5:32). Divorce is evil because it breaks the marriage unity which God planned. When God created Adam and Eve, they became "one flesh" (Gen. 2:24). The one-flesh unity of marriage is a miracle of God's grace. Divorce spoils and destroys the sacred gift of one-flesh unity in marriage. Jesus commanded, "What therefore God has joined together, let no man [separate]" (Matt. 19:6). Jesus said that in the old covenant people were permitted to divorce only because of the "hardness" of their hearts (Matt. 19:8). Divorce should never take place among new covenant people, where the Holy Spirit is present in the life of the believer and the church creating true righteousness (Matt. 5:31-32).

The Bible never specifically prohibits polygamy; nevertheless, most Christian churches do not permit polygamy among their members. Although some men of God in the Old Testament had more than one wife, none of those polygamous marriages is described in the Bible as ideal; in fact, most are described as unhappy. Polygamy spoils the one-flesh union of marriage. One-flesh unity demands total loyalty to one's marriage partner. If a woman or a man has several partners, that spoils that deep inner meaning of marriage as one-flesh union in which the husband is to love his wife as his own body and the wife to respect her husband deeply. In fact the Bible commands the husband to give himself in suffering sacrificial love for his wife just as Christ gave himself in suffering sacrificial love for the church (Eph. 5:21-33).

Truthfulness (Matt. 5:33-37).
The ninth commandment says, "You shall not bear false witness" (Exod. 20:16). Jesus the Messiah pointed out that the inner meaning of this command is that we should not even swear because

those who swear seems to be saying that sometimes they can lie; they are really truthful only when they swear. Truthful persons never have to swear because their word is always true. Truthful people only need to say "yes" or "no" and their associates will know they have told the truth.

Forgiveness (Matt. 5:38-48).

We have mentioned that Jesus taught that the greatest commandment is to love God and the second greatest is to love one's neighbor as oneself. Jesus the Messiah taught that the law of love demands that we forgive our enemies. Although some teachers have said, "An eye for an eye and a tooth for a tooth," Jesus taught Christians to "love your enemies and pray for those who persecute you" (Matt. 5:38, 44). He was very specific, saying that if someone takes your coat, you should give up your shirt as well. If someone slaps you on one cheek, you should turn the other cheek. If your enemies deserve punishment, that is up to God; it is not your responsibility to do evil to your enemy (Rom. 12:19).

Hate and violence create more hate and violence. Taking revenge against enemies does not ease the hate. Only forgiveness can heal the violence. Only love can destroy the hate. If our enemies know we love them, they may become our friends; but if we use violence we will both be hurt and the hate between us will increase.

Riches (Matt. 6:19-34).

The 10th commandment says we should not covet anything our neighbor has. Covetousness is the evil desire to take that which someone else possesses. Our desire for riches and things is the root of covetousness. Jesus taught us to avoid putting trust in riches or possessions. Christians are to seek righteousness; they are to seek first for the kingdom of God. When we love God most of all, he will take care of all our other needs. Jesus said, "Therefore do not be anxious, saying, 'What shall we eat?' or 'What shall we wear?'. . . But seek first his kingdom and his righteousness, and all these things shall be yours as well" (Matt. 6:31, 33).

We cannot include in this short chapter all that Jesus said about the way of righteousness. Probably the most astonishing part of his sermon was when he said, "You, therefore, must be perfect, as your heavenly Father is perfect" (Matt. 5:48)! How can we live as righteously as God? Certainly that kind of righteousness is possible only as the Holy Spirit recreates our lives into the true image and likeness of God. As Jesus said, we can experience that kind of recreation only when we become poor in spirit, when we confess our failure, our sin, and our need for salvation.

Summary

"And when Jesus finished these sayings, the crowds were astonished at his teaching, for he taught them as one who had authority, and not as their scribes" (Matt. 7:28-29).

Christian people are those who recognize the authority of Jesus the Messiah. They submit to God's will by acknowledging Jesus as Lord and Saviour. They are disciples (followers) of Jesus. The first Christians said that those who confessed "Jesus is Lord" were walking in "the way" (Acts 18:26). Even today those who follow Jesus do walk in "the way." This is the way of love, the way Jesus the Messiah lived.

A MUSLIM RESPONSE

The Christian church, unlike the Muslim Umma, has no system of universal law for right conduct. It is the Christians' confessed view that love, which is central to their teaching, cannot be reduced to a set of rules. However, Muslims, who have both a universal divine law and a permanent scheme of revealed moral values, are of the view that man, being imperfect and having limited knowledge, must be guided at all times by this law and moral values. Although man is commanded to practice justice, he does not know how to go about it. So the divine law gives him every detail on how to practice justice and mercy at every instance.

On the other hand, the scheme of moral values on which Christian conduct is based is similar to that of Muslims, although love is made to supersede every other moral value in Christianity. This overstressing of love in all aspects of the Christian life has at times, in Muslim eyes, rendered the Christian ideal of conduct more theoretical than practical.

One practical issue on which Christians and Muslims painfully differ is marriage and divorce. Marriage in Islam is a contract between a man and a woman which is concluded in God's name and is therefore a sacred institution. Everything should be done to uphold this sacred contract.

However, if there are severe obstacles in marriage which cannot be overcome through reconciliation, then Islam, in its practical teachings, has permitted divorce (*talag*). Divorce should be only a last resort. The Prophet Muhammad (PBUH) said, "That of all things permitted by law, divorce is the most hateful in sight of God."[1] Again the Qur'an advises, "If women obey you, then do not seek a way against them."[2] Islam would not tolerate unhappy, faithless, loveless, stagnant marriages. It is for this practical reason that divorce is permitted.

In the same way, forgiveness is recommended as a high moral virtue of Islam, but it must be given in a practical manner. In Islam a wronged or oppressed person has the freedom to resist and retaliate by bringing the offender to book or dealing some punishment for him. He also has the right to forgive the offender, entrusting Allah with the results of his actions. The Qur'an states,

The recompense of an evil deed is punishment proportionate to it, but whoever forgives (the injury caused him thereby) and makes reconciliation, he shall have his reward from Allah. Surely God does not love the wrong doer (Qur'an 42:40).

Another verse says, "Praised are they who restrain their anger and pardon the faults of others; and God loves those who do good to others" (Qur'an 3:134).

Practically in Islam, there is neither the extreme of an eye for an eye, nor the opposite one of turning the left cheek when the right is smitten. There is no giving away the trousers to the brother who has taken away the shirt!

Notes

1. Reported by Son of Omar, Abu Dawd and Hakim, *Fikqi Sunnah*, Vol. 11, (Beirut: by Sayid Sabiq, Daurul-Kitab-l-Alaby), p. 241.
2. Qur'an 4.34.

d he [the Messiah] said to them, "Go into all the world and preach the gospel to the whole creation" (Mark 16:15).

24
The Mission of the Church

THE WORK OF THE CHURCH

Jesus the Messiah began his ministry by proclaiming in the synagogue in Nazareth that the Spirit of the Lord was on him to preach good news to the poor, to proclaim freedom to the captives, to give sight to the blind and liberty to the oppressed (Luke 4:18). This was the announcement that the kingdom of God had begun; in Jesus the Messiah the will of God was perfectly extended into human history. Jesus lived the kingdom; he was the kingdom. People who responded to him in faith received healing in every way: sins were forgiven, the lame walked, the blind saw, the poor received hope. The Messiah was the breakthrough of the kingdom of God into history.

The church is the community of faith which continues that work of God which Jesus began (1 Cor. 12, 13). The church is a continuing sign among the nations that the kingdom of God has begun. Through the presence of the Holy Spirit in the life of the church, the kingdom of God keeps on breaking into our communities and our lives. The church is a sign, a witness in the world that salvation is at hand.

The mission of the church flows out of the experience of redemptive love. Redeemed people are compelled by the love of God to share his love with their fellow human beings. The overflowing love of God in the experience of the church gives Christians a profound urge to serve other people with the same spirit of self-giving love they received from Jesus the Messiah. Christians desire to "walk in love, as Christ loved us and gave himself up for us" (Eph. 5:2). Love for others is at the center of true Christian mission.

How does the church give witness to the presence of the kingdom of God? How does it share God's love with the world? How does it reveal to the world that through Jesus the Messiah God's eternal reign has begun? How does it become a sign to the nations that the redemptive love of God is present, that God's good purpose for history will triumph? The church performs mission in three principal ways.

First, the church performs its mission through fellowship. Those who are members of the church are called by God to love one another (1 Cor. 13). Love was remarkably present at Pentecost, when the church was created. Believers actually sold their possessions and gave all that they had to the poor! We read,

And all who believed were together and had all things in common; and they sold their possessions and goods and distributed them to all, as any had need. And day by day, attending the temple together and breaking bread in their homes, they partook of food with glad and generous hearts, praising God and having favor with all the people. (Acts 2:44-47)

Pentecost was an unusual expression of love. Yet wherever the church is truly faithful, Christians do express love toward one another. Most Christian congregations have ways to share with any believer who suffers misfortune. If a member's house burns down, the believers will take an offering and probably help to rebuild the house. In countless ways Christians in local congregations attempt to show love to one another. They obey the biblical command to "do good to all men, and especially to those who are of the household of faith" (Gal. 6:10).

Christians express love outside the local church. Christians show love to their sisters and brothers in other parts of the world. Each local church is part of the universal Christian church. We have already mentioned that worldwide councils and fellowships represent ways Christians try to show their unity and love. These channels of fellowship flow in many directions. Each Christian denomination is also a fellowship, which normally unites Christians of different nations in a particular denominational family.

Whatever the case may be, the church expresses Christian fellowship in the local situation and across national boundaries. This international fellowship is evident, for example, in the flow of financial assistance from one Christian fellowship to another which has experienced a misfortune such a drought. Another example is hospitality. When we travel, our Christian sisters and brothers in other countries offer us hospitality, even though we are complete strangers. Christian love unites even strangers in fellowship.

Fellowship is the first dimension of Christian mission in the world. It is the love which Christians have for each other. Fellowship is a witness that the kingdom of God has come. Jesus said, "By this all men will know that you are my disciples, if you have love for one another" (John 13:35).

Second, the church performs its mission through service. Perhaps there are Christian churches in your home community. What kinds of service do they perform there? In thousands of communities around the world, the church is involved in a wide variety of social service ministries. On a worldwide basis, some of these ministries include refugee assistance, famine relief, medical ministries, educational development from the primary to university level, desert control and tree planting, agricultural and livestock development, mental health, homes for the aged, housing development, home industries for low-income families, adult literacy, road building, marriage counseling, ministries to delinquent children or to orphans, reading rooms and libraries, disaster reconstruction after floods or earthquakes, exploring new sources of energy, reconciliation when there is conflict between nations, ministry to lepers, trade schools, recreation centers—the list is endless. The church is called by God to be a sign in the community and in the nations that God is concerned, that God does love, that God desires to save us from all that is evil.

Through these ministries of loving service, the church continues the work that Jesus began when he proclaimed the presence of the kingdom of God among people. The church shares the redemptive love of God with others. The church attempts to be a sign of the presence of God's kingdom in history through its ministries of love and service. Wherever there is human need, the church is called to minister, to serve, to express God's love in action.

The church does not believe it can solve all the problems of human need around the world. That is impossible. Societies everywhere experience rebellion against God. Evil is present. But the church is called to be a sign of the kingdom of God, a conscience in society.

An example from Kenya is helpful. Some years ago primary school graduates who could not go on to secondary school had trouble finding jobs. The church recognized the problem and began several polytechnic schools to train primary students in basic technical skills for employment. The ministry was highly successful. Soon society as a whole recognized the value of polytechnics, and today the polytechnic schools are supported by the government. There are countless examples of this. The church in its ministries of social service is a conscience to society, helping to show the path toward more effective humanization. It is a sign of God's loving intention for humankind.

Third, the church performs its mission by proclaiming the gospel throughout the world. Before Jesus went to heaven, he commanded his disciples,

> Go therefore and make disciples of all nations, baptizing them in the name of the Father and of the Son and of the Holy Spirit, teaching them to observe all that I have commanded you; and lo, I am with you always, to the close of the age. (Matt. 28:19-20)

He went on to say, "But you shall receive power when the Holy Spirit has come upon you; and you shall be my witnesses in Jerusalem and in all Judea and Samaria and to end of earth" (Acts 1:8). God commanded the church to take the gospel to the end of the earth. Christians are commanded to preach with urgency, calling on people to repent and to believe in Jesus the Messiah as the Lord and Savior who was sent by God to redeem humankind. They are commanded to baptize and teach the nations and to form new church fellowships among all peoples. Christians call this command the great commission.

After Pentecost, the church began to obey the great commission. In the lifetimes of the apostles, Christian missionaries took the gospel from Palestine into lands hundreds and thousands of miles from Jerusalem. In half a century, Christians baptized believers and formed churches from India in the east to Spain in the west. They also took the gospel to Egypt and other parts of northern Africa.

Sometimes the church has failed to continue or to understand the great commission and has attempted to spread the church through warfare and violence. For example, "Christian" armies "converted" several communities in Europe through conquest. Christians are saddened that during the Crusades in the Middle Ages, Christian armies conquered the Middle East and tried forcefully to convert peoples to Christianity. These are horrible examples of a tragic Christian failure to understand and practice the great commission.

At the same time, many periods in the history of the church have been blessed by multitudes of faithful Christian missionaries who gave their lives to take the gospel to the end of the earth. These days more missionaries are serving around the world than at any time in the history of the Christian church.

The Presbyterian church in Kenya recently sent a missionary to New York. Some Tanzanian Christians are sharing the gospel in China. Japanese missionaries have gone to South America. Pakistani Christians are witnessing in Kuwait. Indian Christians are ministering in Sudan. Hungarian missionaries serve in Kenya. Christians move in all directions from their home church communities, from their local "Jerusalems."

Wherever Christians go they take the gospel. Many of these witnesses are commissioned and sent by their local congregation to a foreign country to proclaim the gospel. Others go for business, professional, or educational reasons, but wherever they go, they should share the gospel.

Of course, the church must remember that proclaiming the gospel needs to begin at home. Faithful Christian congregations attempt to share the gospel with their neighbors first of all. That is always the beginning of mission. But repeatedly Christian congregations also sense the call of the Spirit of God to go beyond the immediate neighborhood to peoples who have never heard the gospel. The Bible reveals that it is God's will that every people on earth hear the gospel before the end of history and that fellowships of believers develop among these peoples (Matt. 24:14; 28:16-20; Acts 1:8; Phil. 2:9-11).

Summary

Christians believe the church is a sign of the kingdom of God which broke into human history through Jesus Christ and the Pentecost event when the Holy Spirit was poured out on the believers. They believe that the mission of the church is to be a sign and a witness among the nations of the presence of the kingdom of God among humankind. As we have mentioned, the church becomes a sign of the kingdom by continuing the work and ministry which Jesus Christ began. This includes fellowship, service, and witness.

The witness of the Bible is that at the end of history Jesus the Messiah will return to earth in glory and the kingdom of God will be fulfilled. At that time the nations and peoples of the earth will be judged. Those who have persisted in their rebellion against God will experience eternal punishment. The earth will pass away and human history will be consummated.

Those who have responded to God's grace and have begun to participate in the kingdom of God will experience eternal salvation. God's reign will be consummated. The kingdom of God which began through the first coming of Jesus the Messiah will be completed and fulfilled. All things in heaven and earth will acknowledge Jesus the Messiah as the one whom God has appointed Lord and Savior. That is God's plan for history (Mark 14:62; Phil. 2:9-11; Rev. 20:11-15; 21:1-8; 22:27).

A MUSLIM RESPONSE

Both Muslims and Christians strive to proclaim "good news" to the world, as commanded by God and exemplified by their respective prophets. The two communities take service as a fundamental duty to humanity, and especially to the community of faith.

However, the two organize their missions differently. Islam, which has no ordained hierarchy of priesthood and no organized missionary orders like Christianity, has been mostly propagated and spread by committed Muslim individuals who have had only limited means of livelihood. It is for this reason that Muslim service, through visible material structures like hospitals, roads, or conference centers, has been conspicuously lacking, especially in areas where Muslims are in the minority. Although Muslims stress preaching, this does not mean that they are only concerned about life in the hereafter. Islam, as a complete way of life, is naturally as much concerned about this life as the life after death. Work and service is a duty enjoined by God and is part of Muslim worship.

Although Islam acknowledges the second coming of the Messiah, the nature of his anticipated mission is different from the Christian anticipation. Muslims believe the Messiah will return to earth to firmly establish the true religion of Islam before the final judgment.

Conclusion

Islam and Christianity are two living faiths which claim to have a mission to the whole of humankind. In this book we have highlighted, albeit briefly, some of the major issues which bring Muslims and Christians together or separate them in their worship of God and witness among their fellow humans.

We the authors are thankful for those beliefs we hold in common. We both recognize the faith of Abraham and seek to understand and live in accordance with the faith he exercised. We believe that faith needs to be enlightened through the witness of prophets, apostles, and the Scriptures. We believe that revelation is not a human invention but the gracious gift of God to human beings. We believe that history has meaning, that it is moving toward a consummation in judgment. We both believe in the resurrection of the dead. We believe that all this springs from God who is the sovereign, transcendent, righteous Creator of all. Each of us believes that God commands his people to witness and invite unbelievers into repentance and into the community of faith. We believe God has established a witnessing community of faith.

While giving thanks for and affirming the faith which unites us, we also confess that our respective witnesses differ in important ways. The Muslim witness is that the Qur'an is God's final and definitive revelation of his perfect will to humankind. The Christian witness is that Jesus the Messiah is the living Word of God in human form. For the Muslim, the Qur'an is the criterion of truth. For the Christian the total biblical witness culminating in Jesus is the criterion of truth. All a Muslim or a Christian believes about humans, God, salvation, guidance, righteousness, revelation, judgment, and community is determined by these commitments.

In our dialogue, we have sensed that there are areas in which our beliefs are complementary. We give thanks for these points of commonality. But at the same time we are aware of significant differences. Islam and Christianity agree that God is merciful, that God loves. The question is how closely God chooses to identify with our human situation. That is the fundamental question: How does God express his love and mercy?

In Islam, God's mercy is supremely expressed through the revelation of a perfect law. In Christian faith, God's love is supremely expressed in the suffering, redemptive love revealed in the life, crucifixion, and resurrection of Jesus the Messiah. These are not superficial differences. They deal with the most fundamental questions of the meaning of human existence. There is no way a Muslim and a Christian can honestly proclaim that these differences are irrelevant or insignificant.

The nature of the theological issues is so exceedingly profound that the questions at stake cannot be appropriately understood or resolved through propositional polemics or logical positivisms. Our conversation in the interest of truth must move on the level of ultimate reality, the reality which probes more deeply than mere rationalism can into the meaning of human existence.

On this we both agree: truth is the *Word* of authoritative revelation from God. That common starting point is both the point of convergence and the point of divergence between us. Is the Word of revelation preeminently a book or supremely evident in a person? That issue cannot be resolved by argument; the very nature of the issue demands patience, listening, and witness by both communities of faith.

Nevertheless, we believe that the pain caused by these differences should not prevent us from continuing conversation. The issues which divide us must not build walls of hostility between us so that the dialogue ceases. If we truly desire truth and a deeper understanding of one another, then our mutual conversation must continue. The conversation should move on many levels. This book has been a written conversation. There are also other levels of conversation which are equally important. Probably the most significant level of conversation should be good neighborliness. We must learn to know one another as friends. We must pray to God, asking him to help us cultivate bridges of love between our communities. We must learn the conversation of love, forgiveness, respect, good neighborliness, listening, and witness.

Amen

Glossary

Islamic terms

abd	the servant or slave of God
Abdallah	Muhammad's (PBUH) father
Abu Bakr	one of the first Muslim believers and also the first Caliph
Abu Talib	Muhammad's (PBUH) uncle
Adam	the father of all people, the husband of Eve (Hauwa) who was the first woman
adhan	call to prayer
Ahl al-Kitab	People of the Book, that is Jews and Christians
al-asma' al husna	the ninety-nine beautiful names of God
Ali	one of the first Muslim believers and also cousin and son-in-law to the Prophet. He became the fourth Caliph
Amina	Muhammad's (PBUH) mother
Ansar	the helpers in Madinah
aya	a verse in the Qur'an
Basmalah	the praise statement which every Muslim must say before doing anything: "In the Name of Allah, the Compassionate, the Merciful" (*Bis-mi-llahi ar-Rahamani ar-Rahim*). All Quranic *surahs* except one begin with the *Basmalah*.
Battle at Badr	Muslims defeated the infidels
Bilal and Khabbab	Muslims who suffered severe persecution in Makkah

the Books of God	the five books which God has sent down to man. The Book revealed through Abraham (*Suhuf*) has been lost. The other four have not been lost.
Din, al-.	religion
Fatiha, al-	the opening chapter of the Qur'an, the perfect prayer for Muslims
fuqaha	Doctors of Islamic law
The Garden	a heavenly paradise above the earth where Adam and Hauwa were placed before they yielded to the temptation of *Iblis*
ghusul	bathing in the prescribed Muslim manner
Hadith	the written traditions concerning the prophet which include both his teachings and practices
haj	the pilgrimage to the Ka'bah
Hauwa	Eve, the mother of all people, the wife of Adam who was the first man
Hafz	Quranic memorizers
Hijrah	the migration from Makkah to Yathreb (Madinah), A.D. 622, the beginning of the Islamic era
Hudaibiyya	the treaty between the Makkan Quraish and the Muslim *Umma*
ibadat	devotional worship and submission
Iblis	Satan who is the source of all evil
ihsan	right conduct
ijima	consensus
Imam	the head of the Shi'a Muslims who traces his geneology to the Prophet
imam	the leader of prayers in the mosque
iman	belief or faith
isnad	the chain of witness through which the *Hadith* has been transmitted
iqra	recite the recitation of Divine revelation
jahiliyya	the time of ignorance in Arabia before the coming of the Prophet Muhammad (PBUH)
Jalil, al-	Most Majestic; one of the names of God

Janna	Paradise, the place Adam and Hauwa first lived and the place to which the true slaves of Allah will return
Jibril	Gabriel, through whom God has sent down His Books to the apostles
jihad	striving in the path of Allah
jinn	a spirit. Some *jinns* are evil and some are good. The evil *jinns* are followers of *Iblis*
Juma	Friday congregational prayer.
Ka'bah	the house of God in Makkah in which there is a sacred black stone toward which all Muslims face when they pray
Khadija	Muhammad's (PBUH) first wife
khalifa	Vicegerent. Man was sent by God to earth to be His *khalifa* or caretaker on earth in obedience to the Divine command
kufr	disbelief and atheism, one of the greatest sins in Islam
Lat, al-	the sun goddess in pre-Islamic Arabia, who was worshiped as one of the three daughters of Allah
Lailat ul-Qadar	the Night of Power when Muhammad (PBUH) received his first revelation
Manat, al-	the goddess of destiny in pre-Islamic Arabia, who was considered to be one of three daughters of Allah
Mir'aj	the ascension of the Prophet (PBUH)
Moses	the Prophet of God through whom the Torah was revealed
mosque	a building in which Muslims gather for prayer
Mount Hira	the place where Muhammad (PBUH) first began to receive revelation
Muhajirun	the emigrants to Madinah
Munafiqun	hypocrite Muslims
nabbi	a prophet of God who proclaims the will of God
Negus, King	Abyssinian Christian King who gave the Muslims refuge

Qibla	the direction of prayer
qiyas	analogical reasoning
Quraish	the tribe of the Prophet Muhammad (PBUH)
Rahim	Most Merciful; one of the names of God
Rahman	Most Gracious; one of the names of God
Ramadhan	the month of fasting
rasul	an apostle of God through whom God reveals a Book
sahaba	Companions of the Prophet Muhammad (PBUH)
salah	the ritual prayer in Islam
saum	fasting
Shahada	the Muslim credal witness: 'There is no god but Allah, and Muhammad is the Apostle of Allah.'
Shari'a	the Law of God
Shi'a	the Muslim community who believe that the head of the community should be a descendant of the Prophet
shirk	associating Allah with other gods, the greatest sin in Islam
Sunnah	the way or practices of the Prophet
Sunni	the Muslim community who look to the Qur'an, *Sunnah*, and community consensus for authority
Surah	a chapter in the Qur'an
taharah	purification
tanzil	the sending down of Books from heaven
'ulama	scholars of Islamic law and theology
'Umar	an early convert to Islam who later became the second Caliph
Umma	the community of Islam
'Uthman	one of the first Muslim believers and also the third Caliph
Uzza, al-	the goddess Venus in pre-Islamic Arabia, who was considered to be one of the three daughters of Allah

Wahay	Divine revelation
wudu	ablution before prayers
zakat	obligatory alms

Christian terms

apostles	leaders of the early church
baptism	a sign with water that a person is accepted into the Christian church
Bethlehem	the Judean town where Jesus was born
bishop	a church leader responsible for a group of Christian congregations
church	the gathered community who believe in Jesus the Messiah as Savior and Lord
covenant	a solemn agreement between two or more persons. God has invited humankind into a covenant of blessing with himself.
deacon	a church leader who assists the minister or bishop
El or Elohim	the name for God used by Abraham. El or Elohim is the Hebrew form of the Arabic name Allah
eucharist or communion	the sharing of bread and wine as a sign of new life and communion experienced through the life, death, and resurrection of Jesus the Messiah
elder	a minister in the early church
Epistles	letters written by apostles to churches
Gabriel	the angel who came to Mary before the birth of Jesus
garden of Eden	the place where Adam and Eve first lived
gospel	good news (*euaggellion* or *injil*) that God has acted redemptively in Jesus the Messiah
great commission	the command of Jesus to his disciples to preach the gospel in the whole world
Herod, King	King of Judea when Jesus was born
I AM	the name for God which was revealed to the prophet Moses at the burning bush
Immanuel	a name for the Messiah which means "God with us"
incarnation	the belief that God has revealed himself in Jesus the Messiah
Jerusalem	the city in which Jesus was crucified

Jerusalem Conference	a Christian conference held in A.D. 43 to discuss the Christian attitude toward culture
John the Baptist	the prophet who baptized and prepared people to receive the Messiah
Joseph	the man who was engaged to Mary when she gave birth to Jesus. He became her husband.
Joseph of Arimathea	a rich man who provided a grave for Jesus
kingdom of God	the rule of God in heaven and earth
Messiah	"the anointed one," the Semitic form of the Greek word *Kristos*, or Christ
Mount Sinai	where God revealed the Ten Commandments
Nazareth	the Galilean town where Jesus grew up
New Testament	the portion of the Bible written after the coming of the Messiah
Old Testament	the portion of the Bible written before the coming of the Messiah
ordain	the way church leaders are commissioned to their task by the bishops or ministers who lay hands on them and pray for the Holy Spirit to give the necessary gifts of leadership
Passover	the feast which reminds the Jewish people of their deliverance from Pharaoh
Paul	one of the apostles who was inspired by God to write portions of the New Testament
Pentecost	Feast of Harvest after Jesus had returned to heaven at which time the Holy Spirit came upon the believers in a special way
people of Israel	the people of the Old Testament covenant
Pharaoh	the king of ancient Egypt
Psalms	poems and hymns, many of which were written by David; known as *Zabur* by Muslims
sacrifice	an offering often given as a sign of one's desire for forgiveness

salvation	the experience of forgiveness of sin and a right and joyous relationship with God
Satan	the devil
Savior	Jesus means the Savior who saves mankind from sin and evil
secular	pertaining to the earth in the present time
Sermon on the Mount	teachings on righteousness given by Jesus to his disciples
shepherds	the people to whom the angels announced the birth of Jesus
Son of God	Messiah who had a perfect relationship with God
Spirit of God	sometimes called the Holy Spirit. God is present among humankind as Spirit.
Taurat	See Torah
Ten Commandments	principles of right conduct which God revealed to the covenant people
testament	a solemn agreement or covenant
Torah	the first five books of the Bible, also called the Pentateuch of the prophet Moses
Trinity	an attempt by Christians to express the unity and love of God as revealed in God as Creator, Savior, and Spirit (Father, Son, Holy Spirit)
virgin Mary	the mother of Jesus
wise men	the men from the East who came to Jerusalem to find the Messiah at the time of his birth
Yahweh	the Hebrew name for God which was revealed to the prophet Moses at the burning bush. This name means "I AM" or "I Will Be" or "I Was." It is God as the one who enters into covenant with humans.

Select Bibliography

al-Ghazali. *Inner Dimensions of Islamic Worship*. Leicester: Islamic Foundation, 1983.

Ali, Abdullah Yusuf. *The Holy Qur'an: Text, Translation, and Commentary*. Delhi: Kutub Isha'at-ul-Islam.

Anderson, J. N. D. *Christianity: The Witness of History*. London: Tyndale Press, 1970.

Anderson, W. B. *The Church in East Africa, 1840-1974*. Dodoma, Tanzania: Central Tanganyika Press, 1977.

Arberry, A. J. *The Koran Interpreted*. New York: Macmillan, 1955.

Azizullah, Muhammad. *Glimpses of the Hadi*. Takoma Park, Md.: The Crescent Publications, 1973.

Brown, David. *The Christian Scriptures*. London: S.P.C.K., 1968.

_____. *The Cross of the Messiah*. London: S.P.C.K., 1969.

Burton, J. *An Introduction to the Hadith*. Edinburgh: Edinburgh University Press, 1994.

Clark, Dennis E. *The Life and Teaching of Jesus the Messiah*. Elgin, Ill.: Dove Publications, 1977.

Cragg, Kenneth. *The Call of the Minaret*. New York, Oxford University Press, 1964.

_____. *The Dome and the Rock*, London: S.P.C.K., 1964.

_____. *The House of Islam*. Encino, Calif.: Dickenson Publishing Co. Inc., 1975.

_____. *Jesus and the Muslim: An Exploration*. London: George Allen and Unwin, 1985.

Cragg, Kenneth and Marston Speight. *Islam From Within: Anthology of a Religion*. Belmont, Calif.: Wadsworth, 1980.

_____. *Muhammad and the Christian, a Question of Response*. Maryknoll: Orbis, 1984.

Dodd, C. H. *The Founder of Christianity*. New York: Macmillan, 1976.

Esposito, John L. *Islam: The Straight Path*. 2nd. ed. Oxford: Oxford University Press, 1991.

_____. editor, *Voices of Resurgent Islam*. New York: Oxford University Press, 1983.

Gaudeul, Jean-Marie. *Encounters and Clashes: Islam and Christianity in History*. 2 vols. Rome: Pontificio Instituto di Studi Arabi e Islamici, 1984.

Gibb, H. A. R. *Islam*. London: Oxford University Press, 1975.

Goddard, Hugh. *Christians and Muslims: From Double Standards to Mutual Understanding*. Surrey: Curzon Press, 1995.

Guillaume, Alfred. *Islam*. Penguin, 1979.

Haddad, Yvonne Yazbeck. *Contemporary Islam and the Challenge of History*. Albany: State University of New York Press, 1980.

Haines, David. *An Introduction to Islam*. Cambridge: Cambridge University Press, 1995.

Hitti, Philip K. *History of the Arabs*. London: Macmillan, 1973.

Holy Bible, The New International Version. Grand Rapids, Mich.: Zondervan Bible Publishers, 1973.

Holy Bible, The, Revised Standard Version. Grand Rapids: Zondervan, 1973.

Hourani, Albert H. *A History of the Arab Peoples*. London: Faber, 1991.

_____. *Islam: Our Choice*. Karachi: Begum Aisha Bawany Waqf, 1970.

_____. *Islam the First and Final Religion*, Karachi: Begum Aisha Bawany Waqf, 1978.

Jomier, J. *Jesus, The Life of the Messiah*, Vaniyayambadi, India: Concordia, 1974.

Kamali, M. H. *Principles of Islamic Jurisprudence*. 2nd. ed. Cambridge: Islamic Texts Society, 1991.

Kealy, John P. and Shenk, David W. *The Early Church and Africa*. Nairobi: Oxford University Press, 1974.

King, Noel Q. *Christian and Muslim in Africa*. New York: Harper & Row, 1971.

Lewis, C. S. *Mere Christianity*. New York, Macmillan, 1960.

Lings, Martin. *Muhammad: His Life Based on the Earliest Sources*. Cambridge: Unwin, 1983.

Maududi, S. Abul Ala. *Finality of Prophethood.* Nairobi: The Islamic Foundation, 1978.

_____. *Fundamentals of Islam.* Nairobi: The Islamic Foundation, 1976.

_____. *Islamic Way of Life.* Nairobi: The Islamic Foundation, 1978.

Miller, Donald G. *The Authority of the Bible.* Grand Rapids, Mich.: Eerdmans, 1972.

Miller, William M. *Beliefs and Practices of the Christians.* Lahore: Masihi Isha'at Khana, 1975.

Newbigin, Lesslie. *The Open Secret.* Grand Rapids, Mich.: Eerdmans, 1978.

Pickthall, Mohammed Marmaduke. *Holy Quran.* New York: The New American Library, 1961.

Qutb, Muhammad. *Islam the Misunderstood Religion.* Kuwait: Ministry of Awqaf and Islamic Affairs, 1964.

Rahman, Fazlur. *Islam.* New York: Holt, Rinehart and Winston, 1966.

_____. *Major Themes of the Qur'an.* Chicago: Bibliotheca Islamica, 1980.

Register, Ray G. *Dialogue and Interfaith Witness with Muslims.* Kingsport, Tenn.: Moody Books, Inc., 1979.

Saulat, Sarwat. *The Life of the Prophet,* Nairobi: Islamic Foundation, 1978.

Shari'at, Ali. *On the Sociology of Islam* (trans. from Persian by Hamid Algar). Berkeley, Calif.: Mizan Press, 1979.

Shenk, David W. *The Holy Book of God: An Introduction.* Accra: A.C.P., 1980.

Sherif, Faruq. *A Guide to the Contents of the Qur'an.* Reading: Garnet Publishing, 1995.

Trimingham, J. Spencer. *Islam in East Africa.* Oxford: Clarendon Press, 1964.

Watt, Montgomery W. *Islamic Creeds: A Selection.* Edinburgh: Edinburgh University Press, 1994.

_____. *Mohammad, Prophet and Statesman.* London: Oxford University Press, 1969.

_____. *Muslim-Christian Encounters: Perceptions and Misperceptions.* London: Routledge, 1991.

The Authors

Badru Kateregga, M.A. (London) was born in the Muslim community of Butambala in Uganda. He was lecturer and head of the Islamic studies unit at Makere University, Uganda. In 1978 he became a lecturer in Islamic studies and comparative religions at Kenyatta University, Nairobi, Kenya. Currently Professor Kateregga is serving as ambassador of the Republic of Uganda in Saudi Arabia and Dean of the Diplomatic Corps in Arabia.

David Shenk, Ph.D. (New York) was born in a Christian missionary home in Tanzania. For ten years he was involved in educational work in Islamic Somalia. Then he worked in Kenya for six years as a lecturer in comparative religion and church history in the Department of Philosophy and Religious Studies at Kenyatta University, Nairobi. Since 1980, Shenk has been based at the Eastern Mennonite Missions headquarters, Salunga, Pennsylvania, where he helps to coordinate interfaith commitments.

Kateregga and Shenk are close friends. Both have been involved for many years in interfaith conversation between Muslims and Christians.